Also Written By Elsie Spittle
Wisdom For Life

Our True Identity

. . .Three Principles

Elsie Spittle

3 Principles for Human Development, Inc
www.3phd.net

About the Author

Elsie Spittle, President of 3 Principles for Human Development, Inc., has been an internationally recognized trainer and consultant for over three decades. She is one of the few people who knew Sydney Banks, originator of the Three Principles, before he had his profound insight, and who stuck by him, despite her own early strong resistance. Elsie had the privilege of receiving "on the job" training directly from Mr. Banks, travelling with him to address mental health practitioners, educators, and others seeking a deeper understanding of life.

Since then, Elsie has been invited to consult with all levels of executives and employees in the corporate world, and has been instrumental in transforming disadvantaged communities. She has worked with staff and youth in juvenile justice settings, as well as with individuals via coaching and retreats, and is co-founder, with Chip Chipman, of the Three Principles School, dedicated to sharing the integrity and purity of the Principles for the benefit of future generations.

In this book, Elsie Spittle shares a collection of heartfelt stories of hope and inspiration. She tells of families and couples coming together with love and understanding, of executives and employees learning to work in harmony, of people who were fighting for survival on the streets, realizing their inner worth and dignity. She also shares her own journey to finding her True Identity.

This collection is a sequel to Ms. Spittle's ***Wisdom for Life***.

What People Are Saying About *Our True Identity*

"Describing her first meetings with Sydney Banks, her initial reactions, and how she finally realized the truth behind what he was saying, Elsie Spittle draws the reader into an extraordinary story—told in a wonderfully ordinary fashion. Once the reader is quite comfortable, Elsie begins giving actual examples of people who are finding insights from within their own wisdom. This touched me deeply.

These stories remind us that beautiful feelings and peace of mind are not dependent on time or circumstances; they do, indeed, exist before time. To the author, I want to say, 'Thank you, thank you, thank you, for writing this book.'"

Gordon Trockman, MD, Psychiatrist
Hawaii

"Elsie has a rare ability to remind us that simple solutions are close at hand, and that problems are only complex because our thinking makes them so. She conveys to the reader, in an easy manner, how to access the truth that clears up mental blockages, allowing creativity and positivity to unfold."

Willy Paterson-Brown, Entrepreneur
Switzerland

"This book is going to help anyone who wants to grow in understanding the essential nature of life and the Principles behind it."

Rita Shuford, PhD, Clinical Psychologist
Hawaii

"In today's increasingly complex and fast-paced world, we are all seeking ways to keep our bearings. It is easy to be led astray and find yourself looking for answers in the wrong places. Elsie shares remarkably simple yet powerful Principles that can help us all find more ease and grace in our lives."

Tim Foley, Human Resources Executive
Fortune 200 Automotive Manufacturing Company
Illinois

"Our True Identity points to the wisdom in each one of us, a wisdom that is unaffected by mental illness, adversity, and pain; a wisdom that helps us live more peacefully and joyfully with all of life's challenges."

Carol A. Paris, MD, Psychiatrist
Maryland

"Have you ever felt there must be some special meaning to your life, but you didn't know what it was? Through an accident of history, this author was the lifelong friend of a man who suddenly became enlightened. On her inner journey, mentored by Sydney Banks, she found her True Identity. Cherish her words. You just might find yourself hidden within."

Keith Blevens, PhD, Clinical Psychologist
Washington

3 Principles For Human Development, Inc.
PO Box 586
Salt Spring Island
BC, V8K 2W2 Canada

website: www.3phd.net

First Printed in 2010
Printed in USA

Library of Congress Catalog Card Number: 2010916962
ISBN-10: 1-456-32486-1
ISBN-13: 978-1-45632-486-5

Psychology / Interpersonal Relations

Editor: Jane Tucker
Book Design and Layout: Tom Tucker
Cover Design: Tom Tucker
Author Photo: Pete Chipman Photography
Cover Illustration: ©iStockphoto.com/Stanislav Pobytov

Tribute

To Sydney Banks, whose profound spiritual insight revealed the Three Principles. Words can never convey the depth of my gratitude for the legacy he has left to me and my family, and to the world. Syd's incomparable wisdom, his unwavering dedication to relieving the suffering of humanity, and his unfailing sense of humor as he observed the world at play, will serve as a beacon to others, for eternity. The Principles he discovered have yet to be fully recognized by the world. Seldom is such a momentous discovery kept so silent for so long. Nonetheless, his work continues to manifest across the wide spectrum of human endeavor.

Note from the Author

"Each chapter is a 'stand-alone' story, meant to be read leisurely, with time to savor and absorb. Sometimes, just a paragraph is enough to prompt an insight from the reader, relating to one's own life. Enjoy!"

Contents

Foreword

Throughout the course of human history, there have been a small handful of human beings who have had an enlightenment experience so deep, so profound, that their message has forever changed the course of history, and the very experience of being human. They were most often ordinary people, no different in any significant way from their contemporaries; and yet, for reasons neither they nor anyone else could comprehend, the wisdom of the ages rushed into their consciousness, giving them a message capable of lifting mankind to a whole new level of understanding of the nature of existence, of the human condition, of compassion, and of the mystical and limitless power of love. Sydney Banks was such a man.

Elsie Spittle and her husband Ken were good friends with Syd and Barb Banks. Syd worked alongside Ken at the local mill before the experience that was to change all their lives, forever. You could say that Elsie was an average housewife living an average life. Her view of life hadn't strayed much from the religious and cultural traditions in which she'd been raised. Life was okay, but there existed a nagging feeling that there must be more. Imagine, for a moment, what it must have been like for Ken and Elsie when their pal told them he'd had a profound experience, in which he came to understand the spiritual nature of life. Right! You would have thought your good friend had gone off of the edge, and they did.

Elsie's initial feelings were just what any of us would have had: shock, confusion and a deep concern about their dear friend's mental state. She was both frustrated and frightened by the strange ways that Syd was now talking, saying things about the meaning of life and God that shook her belief systems to their core. In spite of all this, in spite of her fear and disbelief, in spite of the very world that she perceived at the time, something deep inside was stirring. The part of her that lay before the creation of her belief system was listening. One day, that part of her heard something so profound, it propelled her into a totally new world.

Since that fateful moment, her whole life has been dedicated to sharing this gift with humanity. She was the first to stand with Syd, and share with the world the profound Principles he had discovered. She has had the courage, throughout the years, to over and over again look deep inside and learn. Her wisdom and love have profoundly changed the lives of countless people; not by telling them how to live, but by helping them come to that moment when something deep inside is stirred, when a long forgotten part of them begins to *listen*.

Elsie is an eminently qualified guide to the pearl of wisdom Syd Banks left us all. Read this book slowly, *listen* for a feeling; *listen* without thinking; and perhaps something deep inside will stir. Perhaps something deep inside will listen, and then you will have touched your True Identity.

A.G. "Chip" Chipman, President
Vantage Consulting Group, Inc.

Acknowledgement

Heartfelt thanks to all the people I have had the privilege of working with over the years, personally and professionally. You have shown great courage in looking deep within yourselves and finding the pathway to your True Identity. Sharing insights with you and learning together is the basis of this book. It could not have been written without you.

Special acknowledgement to my husband, who has stood by me through thick and thin. His love and support have steadied me when the path seemed dimly lit; he has rejoiced with me when the light shone brightly. Together we continue our journey.

To my children and their partners, and to my grandchild — my love is with you always.

Preface

Once in a long while, we are gifted with a very special message; a message of hope for humanity. Such a message is contained in this book. Each story has a "map" that shows the reader a path to the treasure found within every living soul, a pathway to our True Identity. When that treasure is uncovered, nuggets of wisdom are revealed, showing us how we can live life to the fullest; how we can live a life of purpose and, in so doing, help ourselves, help those around us, and assist the global community.

Introduction

"There is an answer to life, after all!" This revelation struck me with full force, immediately following my first insight: that my thoughts of anger created my feelings of anger. Thirty-five years ago, when this insight flashed through my mind, it was so profound that it moved me from a feeling of enormous rage to overwhelming gratitude.

I wept with relief and joy. My very being was filled with energy, so much so that I thought my body could not contain it. That insight has never left me. The understanding I gained, that I was the creator of my own experience, transformed my life forever more.

That realization burst open the door of my belief system and exposed my wisdom, my True Self, lying hidden deep within me. My wisdom clearly identified my thinking as the source of my feelings. As my wisdom was uncovered, my thoughts naturally shifted to healthier ones and, consequently, my feelings changed to healthier feelings.

Up to that point, I had believed that my anger was a result of circumstances outside of myself. I had no idea that human beings had the power to think and create experience. Once I saw the innate wisdom in myself, my eyes were opened and I realized that every human being on earth has the same capacity for wisdom and insight.

This insight that there is a direct correlation between the way we think and the way we feel was prompted by the late Sydney Banks, theosopher, author, and human being extraordinaire. Syd shared his profound understanding of the Three Principles that were revealed to him, via insight, in 1973. To say that the transformation in Syd, after his spiritual epiphany, left my husband, Ken and me shaken, is an understatement. Words cannot express how disturbed we were by Syd's message that the Three Principles were the secret to life.

Syd's statement to us, that human beings are gifted with the privilege of creating their own reality, shook us to our very core. Our limited understanding was that life happened, circumstances happened, and we were more or less victims of life's events. In our innocent ignorance, it seemed far easier to believe we were victims, rather than to take responsibility for our lives. We were doing the best we could do, and still life held no great promise.

I used to ponder my life and ask myself, "Is this all there is?" I dearly loved my husband and our two children, yet I felt something missing, some purpose. Without purpose in my life, I became depressed and unhappy, and often took it out on my family. Nothing filled the emptiness. I wondered, "Why are we here?"

The answer came one mystical day. I was feeling particularly morose when I saw Syd and Barb's car coming up our driveway. My first thought was, "Oh no. Not Mr. and Mrs. Pollyanna!" I felt I couldn't stand anymore of their positive attitude toward life. Their relationship had completely transformed after Syd had his spiritual enlightenment. Although I was drawn to the deep feeling I experienced in their presence, I was extremely disturbed by what had happened to Syd.

I remember as if it were yesterday. Syd worked with my husband, Ken, for eight years at a pulp mill located near the city of Nanaimo, in British Columbia. Syd was a welder and Ken was an apprentice pipefitter. Ken often mentioned Syd in conversations about work. He described Scotty, as Syd was referred to at the mill, as a nice man who was quite interesting. He said that Syd was an excellent welder, very skilled and proficient at his trade. Even though Syd and Ken, like the other tradesmen, complained about the work environment and the company, Ken noticed Syd's kindness.

Not all tradesmen had time for the apprentices or shared tools or knowledge with them, but Syd was always willing and helpful.

Syd was a self-taught, natural artist, and painted wonderful pictures. He also hosted a Scottish program on the local radio station. I was intrigued by my husband's description of this man, and when Ken mentioned that Syd might drop in over the weekend, I looked forward to meeting him.

My first encounter with Mr. Banks was not amusing. He brought their new puppy with him. No sooner had he set the puppy down on the floor than it piddled on the carpet. I was rather annoyed, but covered up my dismay as best I could. I chuckle now, remembering how up-tight I was, then. The three of us had tea and discussed life in general. I was taken with our conversation and suggested Syd bring his wife, Barb, over for dinner the following weekend.

From that time on, we became very good friends. I soon considered Barb my best friend. I was impressed by the fact that she was a nurse, and well educated. She was a petite woman with a classic beauty. I admired her gentleness, yet she had a feisty spirit that engaged me. Both she and Syd had a keen sense of humor, and we enjoyed many evenings of laughter.

Together, we would often watch the television series, **Kung Fu**,with David Carradine. We were enthralled with the nuggets of wisdom that Master Po related to Kwai Chang Caine, David Carradine's character, and would expound upon our own theories after the program was over. It was great fun, and at the same time, the nuggets of wisdom lingered and stirred my mind.

The four of us offered to serve as volunteers at the local Crisis Center. I must say, I was very anxious about how I could serve this population. I couldn't really handle my own occasional calamities; how could I possibly help others? But with the encouragement of the Banks', Ken and I gathered our courage in hand and went to the training program for new volunteers. We didn't last long. The traditional techniques the Center used for training didn't engage us. To fall back into someone's arms, to show trust, seemed silly to us. What on earth did that have to do with helping people? I continued to feel insecure about my ability to help others. Syd and Barb were far more comfortable in helping those in need, and were well liked by the staff and clients.

The Banks' mentioned a workshop that was being offered at Cold Mountain, a retreat center situated a couple of hours away. They said the workshop was for self-awareness, and invited us to go with them. Both Ken and I were very reluctant to consider this opportunity. The Banks' decided to go on their own. A couple of days later, I heard that they had cancelled. Then the fateful weekend occurred, and they did make the journey. What happened there was the beginning of a miracle. The rest of the miracle occurred on Salt Spring Island.

Syd tells the story of his Enlightenment on his DVD, called "The Experience", from the DVD set, *The Long Beach Lectures.* I encourage the reader to hear first-hand from Syd what happened to him. What I will share is my perspective of the transformation, as I observed it.

After his spiritual experience, Syd's whole being changed. His face lost years of age, and glowed with an inner light. His body was imbued with spiritual presence; he walked tall, and with confidence. Prior to this, Syd had walked bent over a bit, as if the weight of the world was on his shoulders.

The most significant change in him, as I saw it, was that he talked "funny." Not funny, in terms of humor, but funny as in strange! Syd was not a learned man. He had a grade nine education. He was not well-read, by any stretch of the imagination. Yet after his profound insight, he talked in a way that we had never heard before.

He first told Ken and me of his epiphany a few days after it happened. He described in simple terms what he discovered.

He told us, in a matter-of-fact tone, that he had discovered the secret to life. He told us that he realized what God was, that God was in everyone. He told us that the Three Principles he uncovered would change the fields of psychology and psychiatry. He said he and Barb would travel the world, teaching this to others.

At first, we just listened to Syd as he related what had happened to him. It sounded like a fantasy. It was so beyond our imagination, we thought he had lost his mind. Instead, he had found IT.

Syd worked at the pulp mill for another ten months before he moved his family to Salt Spring. We continued to visit with the Banks'. Life appeared normal, but in reality, was far from it. I would catch myself peering at Syd, trying to see what was so different about him. I would observe Barb, to see how she was taking this turn of events.

Admittedly, at first, Barb was very confused by what had happened to her husband. I appreciated her dilemma. I was also very confused. But she was living with the man. I couldn't imagine what it was like for her, seeing such a dramatic change in the person she'd been married to for so many years. However, in a short time she realized that something extraordinary had occurred, and she stood strong at her husband's side. This distressed me. I felt I had lost my best friend. I felt she had gone to the "other side."

As time went on, I found my curiosity continually aroused. It was an odd time for Ken and me. On one hand, we really enjoyed the Banks' company. On the other hand, we wished they weren't so happy! They were in love with each other in a way we hadn't seen before, and I envied them. They were in love with life. They were incredible parents, showering their children with love and attending to their every need. Their kindness and caring for others was beyond anything I'd ever seen.

I would ask Syd questions about what he had discovered, and he would respond. I found myself challenging him, as he appeared far too confident for my liking. How could he know these things, with his lack of education? I would say to him, "Well, that's just your opinion. Don't you want to hear mine?"

With a gentle look in his eyes, and an enigmatic smile on his face, he would softly say, "No. What I have discovered is not just an opinion. I KNOW this to be so." I became incensed at what I perceived to be his arrogance.

One memorable day, the Banks' stopped by for tea. As we were chatting away, I asked them what they had been up to recently. Syd glanced at Barb; then gazed back at me. "We've been over at the University in Vancouver, talking with the professors of psychology and psychiatry. It was very interesting."

I looked at him, stunned by what he had said. "Surely he must be joking," I thought to myself. "How on earth could a welder, with a grade nine education, be talking to professors? Why, he couldn't even spell psychology!"

My disbelief was so strong that when Barb pulled a brochure out of her handbag, with a photograph of Sydney Banks on the front page, as the presenter at a mental health seminar, I honestly thought they had gone to a quick print shop to have this flyer produced, just to fool me. I thought, "They've gone too far." Yet, the proof was in front of my eyes. The name of the University was on the brochure. The picture was of Syd. How could this be?

My world was crumbling around my feet. Things like this didn't happen in everyday life. I had nothing to hang on to. My dear friends were transforming before my very eyes, and I was at a loss as to what to do.

I recall, vividly, one evening when we invited the Banks' over for dinner. I had prefaced our invitation by saying to Syd, "We would love to have you over for dinner, on the condition that you don't talk any of this nonsense." He chuckled as he replied, "Elsie, you know I don't talk about this to anyone, unless they ask."

The fragrance of the wood smoke, and the sound of the fire crackling in the fireplace, added to the ambiance of our cozy dining room. We were enjoying our dinner, when out of my mouth, without volition, came a question to Syd. "The other day, you were talking about thought, and how we create our reality… What did you mean by that?"

"Do you really want to know?" he asked.

I indignantly responded, "Of course. I wouldn't have asked you if I didn't want to know."

I don't recall exactly what he said. I only remember getting angry at his answer. I also remember saying, "If we really create our reality, I would create a better one than the one I live in now. If life is a bowl of cherries, my life is the pits!"

He burst out laughing, and despite myself, I joined him in the laughter. Soon all four of us were wiping tears of mirth from our eyes. Nonetheless, after they left, Ken and I discussed the change in Syd. We agreed that what had happened to Syd was a mystery. We kept asking ourselves; how does he know about the Principles he talks about? Where did this new knowledge come from? We knew he was minimally educated. We knew he wasn't an avid reader. It continued to be a puzzle as to how he gained the wisdom that was coming out of his mouth.

Then came the magical day I'll never forget, when the Banks' arrived at my door. My state of mind was so low that I couldn't bear to see them. I didn't know what to do. I was in a quandary. We lived in a rural area, so we left our doors unlocked. The procedure was to knock, and enter. I knew they would follow the usual practice, so to avoid meeting them, I hid in the bathroom. I felt safe there. I listened to them enter and call out, "Elsie, are you home?" I stayed silent. Then I heard the door close as they left. Something propelled me out of the bathroom. I went to the back door, facing the driveway, and beckoned them back inside. I was so uneasy in their presence that I couldn't even invite them to sit down and have a cup of tea.

Syd took one look at my distressed face, put his arm around my shoulder, and in the gentlest, most loving manner, said, "Dearie, you'll be okay. God is within you, and everyone. You'll be okay, Dearie."

Hearing those words freaked me out. I almost pushed the Banks' out of our home. I was enraged. How could he say that? From my religious background, I was taught that God is something outside of us. I couldn't fathom what Syd meant. I called a friend on the phone, who also knew Syd. I regaled her with the latest statement from Syd, ranting and raving in my discourse. Usually, she agreed with me, and added fuel to the fire. This time, for some reason, she just listened. Then she said, "Elsie, I've never heard you so upset. You should listen to yourself."

I was furious at her lack of sympathy, and slammed the phone down, thinking to myself, "Fine friend she turned out to be." I walked away from the phone, and sat down to mull over the latest developments with Syd. At that moment, I felt a spark of lucidity and a thought popped into my head. I realized that "Thought creates feeling." I felt a rush of overwhelming relief sweep over me. In that moment, I knew that there was, indeed, an answer to life's dilemmas. I knew there must be more to life then what I had been seeing. I knew that Syd had found something beyond anything I had ever heard of, or even imagined.

Barb told me later that when they were driving away from our home that day, she'd said to Syd, "I guess that's it for our friendship with Ken and Elsie."

Syd replied, "No, Pet. Elsie heard something today."

Barb retorted, "She did? She sure had a funny way of showing it. She just about pushed us out the door!"

I called Syd later that evening, to share with him what I had realized. I thanked him for his unbelievable kindness and patience. I told him how grateful I was that he had not given up on me, despite my challenging him so many times. I told him that I still didn't understand what had happened to him. It was a mystery to me, but I knew it was an extraordinary event. He was deeply moved by my call. He agreed that what had happened to him was a mystical experience, far beyond the understanding of the human intellect.

He told me that Ken and I would travel the world, sharing the miracle we had seen happen to Syd. He told us that we would be talking to people from all walks of life about what we had learned. I acknowledge that this was hard for me to believe at the time. Yet what he predicted has come to pass.

For me, the journey to a fulfilling life began with that first insight into the power of Thought, seeing that our thoughts create our feelings. This insight showed me purpose, illuminating the power and potential of human beings. I felt a glimmer of understanding that why we are here on this earth is to fulfill our potential, knowing that we will never come to the end of our learning, knowing that infinity speaks to continual learning and growing, contributing to the vitality of life. This I know: our life is what we make it. Join me in discovering the eternal pathway to our birthright, to discovering who and what we really are, to uncovering our True Identity.

Accepting Your True Identity

Allow me to introduce you to your True Self; the inner you, the divine spark within all humanity that is perfect. Not everyone knows about their own True Self. If you have met before, that is wonderful. If you have not had the pleasure, let me say that you are in for a treat.

Another way of talking about True Self is saying that everyone is blessed with innate mental health. Do we utilize our mental health to the fullest? I think not. The spiritual process of discovering that we do have this inherent gift within us is an ongoing development.

What is so remarkable about discovering our true nature, is that we don't have to "try" to improve ourselves or "try" to do better. Once we realize we have this divine spark within us, we automatically begin to change for the better. Effortless change is part of the package, the gift we are born with. If change is hard, it is because our ego belief system will not take a back seat. Our birthright is to enjoy life, the best we can, in all its manifestations.

You might say, "What if I'm in prison? How can I possibly enjoy life while I'm incarcerated?" Someone else might ask, "What about the homeless? How can they possibly enjoy life while living in a cardboard box on the street?"

To respond to both questions, let me tell you a story. I worked with the homeless for over four years in downtown Los Angeles, in the heart of skid row. I saw miracles take place there. I saw love and respect blossom on the streets, between the staff of the organization I worked with and the street people.

I observed the staff come up with creative ideas on how to reach out to the homeless in an unusual way. Rather than continuing to meet people with clipboard in hand, asking questions about what they were up to, and how the staff could be of service, they took a different path.

The service providers intuitively felt that the population they were serving wanted to be treated as ordinary folks, not labeled as homeless, and therefore often patronized. Several of the staff had once been on the streets themselves, and knew what it felt like. But prior to the Three Principles education, the helpers were unsure of how to accomplish this. How do you help people who clearly are struggling to survive, while still preserving their dignity?

Before the staff learned that everyone is born with purity of soul, they tended to treat the behavior they observed. As they began to access their own inner wisdom, they saw beyond the behavior, to the individual's core of mental health, and welcomed people from that understanding.

They decided to offer a karaoke evening, serving coffee, donuts, and love. People responded cautiously at first, then more enthusiastically as they felt the unconditional love from the staff. The staff didn't teach their guests the Principles. By this time, the providers' understanding of who we really are had stabilized their own lives considerably. They were well grounded in their mental health; they lived more of the time in deep feelings of appreciation for what they had found as individuals. The deep feeling was all encompassing, and drew the street people to them in droves.

I saw the homeless treated with dignity, and I saw how they responded to that treatment. I saw many of them come to life, mentally and physically, thriving on the love and positive attention shared with them by staff. I saw that as the staff uncovered their own True Identity, that spark of divinity, they saw it in everyone else. This "seeing" drew out the innate mental health in the people they worked with: their colleagues, their families, and the people on the streets, trying to get back on their feet and get their life in order again.

I saw a man who had been on the streets for 30 years, lying on the sidewalk, covered in filth, incoherent with drug use and malnutrition. In a short time, once the staff had connected with him by seeing beyond his behavior to his divine core, a miraculous transformation occurred. He appeared on a video tape dressed in a sport coat, shirt and tie; his appearance and demeanor were healthy, and he was well spoken as he shared the dramatic changes that had taken place in him. He stated on the tape how much he appreciated the staff, who had treated him with respect and love and had never given up on him. "They gave me hope", he said, "and I began to feel alive again." He had found his True Self.

We never lose this gift. It may lie dormant, but we never lose it. If you take a moment to reflect on the wonder of this gift, it will open your eyes and your heart and release the wisdom contained within.

I have had people who are incarcerated tell me they are grateful because they learned about the Principles while in jail, and thus were able to change the habits of thought and behavior that had imprisoned them. I see that many of these people are less incarcerated mentally then many so-called successful people who are "in the free".

I've had people on the streets tell me they are grateful for the cardboard box they have, their simple home that provides some semblance of privacy, preserving their dignity. I see the dignity reflected on their faces, as they find hope that it's never too late to discover their True Self.

I've only shared two examples of populations that have been helped by discovering their true nature. You can extrapolate the Three Principles learning to every human being. You could be a housewife, depressed and without purpose in your life, as I was. You could be a successful business executive, struggling with depression, despite the success. You could be a student, brought up by parents innocently driven by achievement, and innocently passing on the same standards to you. You could be a child, diagnosed with ADD, lovingly supported by family doing the best they can. When parents discover their True Identity, they tend to see beyond their child's diagnosis and see instead the child's divine spark. This seeing makes an enormous difference in how they treat the child.

The message that Sydney Banks left us is profound in its simplicity. We all have the innate, spiritual power to create our individual experience in life. By using this power wisely, we help ourselves, we touch others, and the gift is shared with humanity effortlessly as we travel this epic journey together.

Subtle Learning

Imagine a cold, snowy morning when the temperature is freezing. You get up to turn on the heat and make the coffee, and if you're lucky, take your coffee back to bed with you. The warmth of the eiderdown quilt enfolds you as you snuggle into it, and heat seeps into your body. Your body and soul are content, and you luxuriate in the comfort.

Now, imagine wisdom seeping into your life, from deep in the unexplored depths of your soul. You have an insight, sometimes so subtle that you miss it, like a feather in the wind. Yet you know that something is different. There is a different feeling that you experience, one that you can't define; but nonetheless, a feeling that something has shifted in your psyche.

So what do we tend to do at times like this? Analyze! That's right, you heard me. Analyze! What happened to us? What did we learn? What does it mean? How will it help us? Who can I ask? Who can I tell?

Isn't it interesting how habitual our personal thoughts can be, ready in an instant to take over, to judge and assess an insight when we are privileged to receive one from within ourselves.

Sometimes an insight will be strong and powerful. You know without a doubt that your understanding of life and how experience is created has deepened. At other times, an insight can be so subtle it is difficult to trust that the knowledge revealed has lasting value, and that other insights will occur.

The ability to have insights is inherent. An insight, once experienced, will manifest in its own time, in a way that is right and appropriate to meet one's individual needs. It is natural for the human intellect to try and stay on top of things, to figure out why, where, when and so forth. The feeling of the insight is so good that our personal thinking wants to cling to it, to hang on to the peak experience, longing for an impossible perfection, for more of a good thing, not trusting that more insights will occur.

To let wisdom expand at its own pace sometimes feels like a subtle unfolding that leaves us mystified, and at times bemused. We know we got something, but can't quite hang our hat on what we learned.

Sometimes wisdom feels like an explosion, filling our being with new thoughts that are enlightening. Sometimes an insight can appear as ordinary common sense, and we wonder why we didn't think of it before. We do our best to live with this ambiguity of subtlety and of explosion. There are many and varied depths of insights sharing the same spiritual essence of Mind.

Charles, a young man who spent some time with me in a coaching program, was experiencing such a time of subtle learning. Charles travelled to the island where I live, and the evening he arrived we met for dinner at a local seaside restaurant. The young man was rather nervous initially, but as we perused the menu and I described some of the places to explore on the island, he relaxed and started to notice his surroundings, commenting on the stunning ocean view. We enjoyed our delicious dinner, and soon Charles was sharing with me his concerns about the slow pace of his learning.

"I really am taken with the Three Principles," he stated. "They make complete sense to me, and I am beginning to see life differently since I realized that we create our own reality. But I want to go deeper, to understand more. The first insight I had was very powerful, but since then my learning seems so gradual. I wonder if I am doing something wrong?"

The young man's earnest inquiry touched my heart as I remembered the many times I'd felt the same way; impatient for more understanding, and not appreciating what I had already learned. Always on edge, striving for more, not content with what is, always seeking what isn't.

We talked about the value of appreciating what is rather than yearning for what isn't. My young client wasn't enamored with this discussion. He was impatient for more. My curiosity was aroused. "What are you looking for?" I asked Charles.

"I want to know how to let go of my past. There are things that I've done in the past that trouble me, and I can't seem to let go of this habitual pattern of thought. I have learned about thought recognition but it doesn't seem to help me."

"What do you mean by *thought recognition*?"

"Well," Charles said thoughtfully, "I recognize that I am thinking negatively and when I start to figure out why, I get gripped by my thinking and can't stop the cycle of feeling bad."

"Perhaps what would be helpful is if you ***realized*** the power of Thought rather than just recognizing your thoughts."

"I don't understand." Charles shook his head, looking confused. "I thought recognizing thought was a very insightful concept."

"It is, to a certain degree. When people first begin to explore the principle of Thought, the simple recognition ***that we think*** is powerful. However, the down side is that often people can and do get caught up in analyzing their thinking, rather than realizing the power of Thought to create our experience. The intention of "recognizing thought" may be pure; the reality can be fraught with pitfalls, such as getting mired in figuring out why and what we are thinking, rather than appreciating the fact that we think. By realizing the spiritual power of Thought, versus getting into the content of thought, you will make your reality a mentally healthier one."

The young man was silent for some time as he considered our conversation. We paid our bill and walked out the door into the cold, clear evening. The stars twinkled brightly overhead as we paused and inhaled the crisp air. We walked back toward his hotel, and Charles spoke slowly, as if he were feeling his way with the words he wished to express.

"It seems to me, the more I realize the ***power*** of Thought, the more I will deepen my understanding. It also seems to me that the past won't have such a tenacious hold on me if I ***realize*** that I have the power to think and appreciate the wonder of this gift, rather than being so concerned with the content of my thinking. I'm beginning to appreciate the subtle aspect of wisdom."

We chuckled together. I knew by Charles' thoughtfulness that this realization was life changing for him. "Another thing that occurs to me," he went on, "is that when wisdom is realized, it does away with the barriers that our personal, ego driven thinking can put in the way of our progress. Yes, I see that realizing wisdom neutralizes a troubled past."

Seeing Mental Distractions

Do you ever judge yourself when you find you are engaged in old habits of thinking—habits of insecurity that distract you from enjoying life to the fullest? If you answered 'Yes,' then you belong to one of the biggest clubs in the world. If you answered 'No' then I'd like to learn what you know.

It's not uncommon for people who have learned about the Three Principles to believe that once you learn about Thought, and how you use the power of the Principles to create your world of experience, you should always be able to move away from negative, hurtful thinking.

On one hand, it is true that learning about the Principles helps one make wiser choices about how much attention you give to certain thoughts. For example, when a negative thought pops into your mind, you will realize there is a negative feeling associated with that thought. Because you are wise to the process of creating your own experience, you will be able to move away more easily from that thought, and feel better.

On the other hand, there are still the ups and downs of life, and a variety of emotions to experience. If you observe the variations, the subtle ebb and flow of life, in the same way that you observe the ebb and flow of the ocean tide, you will be less stressed when the flow of life may become dramatic and stormy. By not harboring judgmental thoughts, you will experience a more neutral state of mind; you will experience your True Self.

My experience is this: as you deepen your grounding in the Principles, your true spiritual identity emerges, unhealthy thinking automatically dissipates, and the times of well-being increase, so that, more of the time, you live in a productive and contented world.

Nevertheless, there are times when an unhealthy thought crosses your mind and you end up holding on to it, examining it, and before long you are gripped by habitual thinking, to your own detriment. Those thoughts can be so subtle and well hidden that you might not even be aware of them. You just may not be feeling like yourself, not feeling healthy, and not sure why.

The most helpful solution I've found to moving past the stagnation is to be grateful for ***seeing*** the mental distraction. Even when I'm still gripped by my thinking, I find there is not the same intensity of emotion. There is a feeling of perspective, an underlying ***knowing*** that I am the thinker. That ***knowing*** is your True Self protecting you from too much distress. The feeling still may not be peaceful or pleasant. As a matter of fact, it may be somewhat disconcerting; but because you have more perspective, you are not as unnerved or rattled by your mental discomfort. You have more equilibrium, so the uneasiness is not as potent.

I'm not suggesting that you linger with your discomfort. What I'm pointing to is that your understanding of your True Identity and the spiritual nature of the Principles provides a cushion, which protects you when you do have a bout with mental distraction. Seeing the distraction as another experience to learn from allows you to view the experience, and the feelings attached to it, with neutrality, without judgment against yourself or others. You view the information simply as data. The cushion of understanding allows you to bounce back to mental health.

Perspective brings a wonderful feeling of freedom and liberation. Imagine not having to be concerned about old psychological patterns anymore. Imagine the weight that is taken off your shoulders, from expectations of yourself and of others. Isn't it remarkable that the moment you feel grateful for seeing your mental confusion, you move back toward your innate mental health, rather than judging yourself and remaining in turmoil? What a gift this is…and all because you've learned the fundamentals of creating experience.

Let me share a story with you. Ken and I were invited to a large gathering recently where I knew only the host, having never met his wife. After greeting us and making social conversation, the couple introduced us to several people. Then the doorbell rang, and they moved to welcome other visitors. Ken was acquainted with a few at the party so we joined their conversation. I found myself becoming tense and insecure as memories stirred, and old habits emerged that I had not experienced in quite some time. I was rather taken aback and uncomfortable.

Normally, I love to meet new people, have no difficulty talking with them and delight in finding out more about who they are and what their interests might be. At this moment in time, however, I was not experiencing enjoyment at all. I found myself tongue tied and struggling to make conversation, just as I had years ago whenever I was with a new group of people in a social setting. All my old insecurities emerged, and I sought out a sofa in a corner in which to hide.

While sitting quietly for a few minutes, I regained my balance, was able to calm down, compose myself, and realize what was going on. It was a surprise to relive the old feelings again, and suddenly I felt the humor of the situation. Here I was, usually at ease in situations like this, and for some reason I had found myself in an old television movie of my life. I decided to change the channel.

As I gained perspective, a grateful feeling welled up in me. Feeling more comfortable, I began to make conversation with those around me. Soon I found myself in the thick of things and enjoying myself very much. I caught Ken's eye across the room and we exchanged smiles. I was so pleased to be there, meeting interesting people, finding out new things about our community and making new friends. Had my old patterns of thinking maintained their hold on me, as they had in the old days, I would have missed this lovely gathering.

Upon reflection, what was so appealing to me was that at no time did I ***try*** to do better, berate or judge myself. I just ***noticed*** my insecurity and in the noticing, my personal thinking eased its hold, and before long my anxiety was gone. The Principle of Consciousness was doing its job by helping me become more aware. The Principle of Thought was at its most productive in creating a nicer feeling of ease. The Principle of Mind brought it all together by the wisdom of knowing not to try to be better, just to relax, be still and ***be***.

Mental distraction often plays a significant role in the workplace. It is very helpful to realize that you can be grateful for seeing this, rather than feeling upset because you may be experiencing such distraction. I've had many clients share their concerns with me about this dilemma.

During our regular coaching call, Greg, a senior executive, lamented, "I'm off on a business trip tomorrow to market a new product. It's an excellent design that we're all very proud of, and I'm eager to showcase it to our new client. I don't have much time to talk now as I'm feeling a little harried and distracted. I'm not sure why. I'm usually calm and collected, yet I find myself fretting about mindless things. I was abrupt with my wife this morning because she didn't pick up my shirts at the cleaner's when really, it was my job and I had forgotten. After I arrived at work I snapped at my assistant, demanding a report that wasn't due until the afternoon. I find myself in old habits that I thought I'd moved past. I'm disappointed in myself because I should know better."

As we talked, it became apparent that Greg was more concerned about the upcoming meeting with his new client that he had thought. Once Greg acknowledged he had some insecure thinking about the matter, he was able to relax and see it as nothing more than personal thinking and ego, getting in the way of his being the best he could be.

Greg was feeling rather embarrassed admitting that he could still have insecure thoughts, given that he was a very successful business executive. There was a momentary pause after he shared that thought with me. "I didn't realize that I still harbored strong resistance to the notion that I can be insecure, which is my ego coming into play. I've always thought of myself as a strong individual, very focused and sure of what I want. I don't usually entertain insecure thoughts. These thoughts have been very subtle. It just occurred to me now that my resistance meant there was something there for me to look at.

"Elsie, I must admit, when you said 'Be grateful for seeing your mental habits,' I thought this time you were way off the mark. That was too much to ask. Yet now it makes sense. What point is there in learning about the Principles if seeing your mental habits come to light makes you feel badly? The whole idea is to be able to see past your habits and learn something new."

Nourishment for the Soul

Something that a client said to me resonated very deeply. We were discussing the value of reflection and how often we shortchange ourselves of this beneficial gift.

My client said, "I used to think that reflection was a time to assess myself to see how I could do better. Inevitably I would end up judging myself, and would feel worse. The last time we talked, you mentioned the power of contemplation, and how in that state we touch our soul, our divine spark. That conversation really struck home. Since we spoke, I find that I offer myself time to reflect.

"It may be while I'm driving or walking, working out, whatever. It doesn't really matter what I'm doing. What matters is that now, the ***feeling*** of reflection is different from when I used to reflect to judge myself. Then, it was an effortful feeling, a feeling of ***doing*** reflection rather than ***being*** reflective. I realize now that I wasn't reflecting; I was analyzing. That insight has made a world of difference to me.

"I find that I have more patience and time for in-depth conversations with my colleagues, family and friends, because I see the divine spark in them as well as myself. There isn't a tendency to judge others so much, and I realize that I don't focus on their behavior like I used to. I was very conscious of people's behavior, and often found it annoying. Now that I see folks with more understanding and compassion, my life is so much more enjoyable."

There were several points that registered with me about what my client, a young woman, said. Her statement, "I offer myself time to reflect," lingered with me. How wise to take the time, and to acknowledge the results of reflection.

We take time to eat, to exercise, to rest; seldom do we take time to nourish the soul. Surely that is what reflection does.

Reflection brings the soul to life, allowing that divine spark to manifest. I also appreciated the young woman's understanding of the difference in the feeling of reflection. How many times in the past had I persistently ruminated over a problem even though I found no answer, because I thought rumination was reflection. I didn't realize that the feeling was effortful. I was so used to a busy mind, and so used to effort, that it seemed natural, and what I assumed reflection was meant to be.

It wasn't until I experienced a deeper level of connection with my inner self, a feeling that is peaceful and at the same time energizing, informative and fascinating, that I knew what I had experienced before was personal cogitation. The deeper reflection is communion with Mind. I know that may sound esoteric; nonetheless, that is what comes to mind to try and describe the indescribable.

There are many varied beliefs, reflecting the many cultures in the world. I've heard it said there are different kinds of souls; that a Caucasian soul is different from a Black, Asian, Indian, Muslim or Jewish soul, or a soul of any other ethnicity. In my opinion, this is nonsense. Soul is divine, pure spiritual energy.

It seems to me that if we are all made from the same essence, the same spiritual energy, then it follows that underneath the disguise of different cultures lies Divine Soul. Spiritual energy provides commonalities among the races, not differences. The commonality is what brings about understanding and harmony, rather than contention. How liberating to see the ***essence*** of individuals, while at the same time respecting and celebrating their individuality.

Trying to describe soul is impossible. The closest I can come to describing soul is a ***sensing*** that there is something beyond the physical form. In the book *The Enlightened Gardener,*

Sydney Banks describes soul as "pure Consciousness." "Rediscovering Mind and Soul", Chapter 11, is a remarkable chapter. If you haven't had the pleasure of reading this book, please do so. There is no clearer description of Mind and Soul.

What I've discovered is that when you nourish your soul, your listening is automatically enhanced. You are more in alignment, and therefore listening to your soul, to Consciousness.

An illustration of how this works comes to mind. A client by the name of Amanda called me, seeking advice, and I did my best to accommodate her. A few days later, she told me she hadn't found my advice helpful. Amanda stated that she didn't wish to disagree with me, and then promptly disagreed.

My ego fell for this maneuver, hook, line and sinker. I had gone over the edge and gotten involved in my client's thinking, rather than pointing her back inside where her own wisdom resided. I felt compelled to retaliate, and had to bite my tongue. During this bit of provocation, the thoughts going through my head were: "She asks for my help; then doesn't take it." "She's stuck in her beliefs and doesn't want to listen." "I can't be bothered with this nonsense."

At this point, I realized the best thing to do was nothing, as I also was gripped by old patterns of thinking. We agreed to talk again in a couple of weeks. Doing nothing, allowing some space for insight, proved to be the saving grace for me. In the past, I would have blindly follow my compelling thoughts and been very direct in my comments, speaking without respect. Of course, the lack of respect would have aggravated the situation, inflicting distress on whomever I was involved with, and on myself.

I have learned not to follow the thoughts that do not serve me well. I have more faith to be still and to quiet my mind, trusting that my innate health will rise to the surface once again. This has taught me patience, and has elicited more attentive listening to my inner wisdom and to others'.

Two weeks passed and I heard from Amanda again. This time the interaction was kind and thoughtful. From our conversation, I learned that Amanda had turned inward and searched within herself, coming up with her own answers, prompting a deeper understanding of her own innate resources. She was apologetic for being, in her words, "quite contrary." I shared what I had discovered about my own ego, and also how I had realized that her thinking was none of my business. What was my business was recognizing, and reminding her of, her True Identity. The dialogue brought us closer, seeing in each other our common humanity and beyond that, our spiritual being.

What occurred to me from this experience was that listening to my wisdom and being still contributed to Amanda having the opportunity to hear her own wisdom. Had I pursued the conversation that my ego was prompting, more than likely the situation would have put her off and engaged her self-image. Finding the stillness within cleared the way for Divine Mind to work gently and nudge both of us to greater understanding.

A Clear Path to Efficiency

Frequently, clients ask me how they can share their understanding of the Three Principles in the workplace. They have many "how to" questions. It is difficult to give cut and dried answers, as each situation is different, and it is best for the individual to contemplate his or her own wisdom for solutions. However, I will attempt to respond, in broad terms, in the hope that it may prompt insight on the reader's part.

How do we educate others about the difference between the Three Principles understanding and traditional programs, where the focus tends to be on behavior, as opposed to what creates behavior? How do we illustrate that these Principles are useful for goal-oriented organizations? How do we present the Principles in a way that is understandable? How do we talk about "feelings and tone" to the work force in a way that is practical and relevant to their work and to the bottom line?

First of all, there is no specific technique to sharing your understanding. The fact that there is no technique to acquire wisdom is part of what is new and exciting about the Principles. The spiritual fact is that the Principles are inherent in everyone; when you realize this, your common sense or wisdom is released. At this point, you naturally employ the Principles in the most productive, healthy way.

If you have been touched by the Principles on a personal level, that above all else is worth its weight in gold. You will have experienced the impact of your own innate health, and seen the results of that power. This experience provides you with a level of certainty and calmness that will arouse the curiosity of your workmates. There is no need to convince anyone of the Principles. First of all, it is impossible to do so.

Secondly, if you try to convince someone of the validity of this understanding, it is liable to put the person off, producing a less than positive reaction. In other words, you will get "push-back."

The best way to share is to just be you, and do what makes sense in the moment. I know that may sound naïve and simplistic; however, it is the simple elegance and the deep feeling that accompanies the Three Principles understanding that attracts most people. There is a science, and an undeniable logic to the Principles. It shows up in the results that occur when human beings operate from their wisdom. Wisdom infuses people with warmth, vitality and calmness that seems out of the ordinary; and yet, at the same time, is very ordinary.

What I've observed and experienced is that people are attracted to these healthy qualities, and will become curious and inquire about your philosophy of life. If they remain interested, they will have questions about how you learned to live this way. The best "sharing" is living what you know; living from the state of gratitude where you see life as a gift. As your behavior changes because you are thinking differently, more positively, your interactions with others will change for the better. That change is what arouses people's interest.

Letting co-workers know that this approach is uniquely different provides an opportunity for you to reflect on the Principles as the foundation for human behavior. There are a vast array of leadership and business books, offering a multitude of techniques and approaches to a better, more successful work life. To read through all this material is impossible, and I think people do get tired of constantly searching for new and better ways of getting ahead.

Isn't it great to realize that wisdom exists in you, an infinite resource where you will find a limitless supply of common sense, always appropriate for your particular needs at any time? I would say this is unique to the Principles:

knowing you create your reality, ***knowing*** that you can stop the search, ***knowing*** the journey is endless and infinite and ***knowing*** it's an inner journey. What a relief to see that we don't have to keep learning new techniques on how to move forward in life! That all we have to do is draw on our innate health, and our life will naturally become better, and continue to improve as time progresses.

Sometimes, people think that if you stop the search, life will be boring; that there is nothing new to discover without buying yet another "how to succeed in business" volume. Nothing could be further from the truth. When you tap into spiritual wisdom, you, metaphorically speaking, have the Library of Congress and all the great libraries of the world and beyond, at your fingertips. Insights and practical information will unfold for you consistently, unendingly. How fascinating is that—the opportunity to tune into never-ending originality?

Another point that is distinct in this approach is that the power of the Principles allows us to create our personal reality. Many discourses have been written on changing behavior. But to change behavior, or the form of reality, ***before*** form takes place is something new. The spiritual fact is that as our thinking gets healthier, so does our behavior. In other words, when negative thinking ceases, negative behavior is not created.

I have read tomes of enlightenment that talk about thought, awareness, and mind, each as a separate issue. I have not seen the Three Principles so clearly described as unified, as working in harmony to produce the human experience, as I have in Sydney Banks' work. This, too, is a point of distinction. To know that the Three Principles generate human experience, regardless of education, religion, income, or ethnicity, is the foundation for human development.

Sharing the positive changes you have observed, in other individuals and in yourself, is helpful when describing the practicality of the Principles to your co-workers. Superior work performance is the most practical, cost effective route to improving the bottom line, and who doesn't want to hear about an enhanced bottom line? In financial terms, in terms of increased production and better service, all will benefit from a calm and cogent state of mind.

The logic of clear thinking lends itself to improved results. The question that arises is how do we achieve a clear state of mind? And that question provides an opening to explore in more depth, with your organization, the power and the impact of the Principles.

The beauty of sharing your understanding with others is that it gives you endless opportunities to deepen your own understanding. You learn so much from other individuals that you are continually in a "learning and growing" position. How can you beat that for self-development?

Being able to articulate the Principles in a way that is pertinent to your organization's needs depends a great deal on your listening aptitude. The ability to listen with a quiet mind establishes relevance and is a key element to being in service. It helps bridge the gap between what the organization knows about human relations and what you know, and allows you to bring the Principles down to earth in a way that makes sense to them. Quiet observation and listening offer you new ways of describing the dynamics of the Principles in terms that are understandable. In doing so, you will expand how you yourself see the Principles. Quiet listening will deepen your understanding of your colleagues' world.

Quiet listening means listening without mental distractions on your mind, so that you hear very deeply. It is a quality of listening that is in tune with what is being said, beyond the words; being sensitive to the feeling that is coming from those with whom you are speaking. It is being in a state of mind where you are not worrying about what to say, trusting that you will know what to do, and that questions will occur to you that will draw the best from the individual or group. Another way of describing quiet listening is: to be in the moment, to be calmly present.

An example comes to mind. A client had requested feedback from me, pertaining to himself and his organization. I asked him if I could be direct, and he responded, "Certainly." Although I had strong rapport with this client, in that instance I knew he probably would not like what I had to say, and my feeling was to wait. Instead, however, I went ahead and shared with him my observations of how I saw him avoiding issues at work that were contributing to low morale in his department. He immediately took umbrage at what I had said, and gave me his reasons for avoiding these work related issues. Suffice to say, the meeting was not a success, and I left thinking that he wasn't very open.

It wasn't until later, after I had time to reflect, that it occurred to me that I was the one who had not been open to listening to him. Had I been more aware at the time, and paid attention to both my feeling and the feeling of unease emanating from him, I would have been more patient, listened more deeply, and realized that once again I was getting involved in the content of his thinking versus his power to think. I would have trusted that another way of reaching him would have occurred to me. Ego-compelling thoughts moved me to "fix" him and I fell into a pit of my own making.

After a week or so, I contacted him and shared that I felt I had been less than sensitive to his needs. That expression of honesty paved the way for a deeper discussion. We explored the nature of the Principles, rather than what the Principles do. Our spirits soared as we touched on this topic. Later, he told me that after this conversation he was elated, and new ideas occurred to him on how to help his employees. He realized he could be more responsive to the low morale by inviting a cross section of employees to meet with him, and to come up with strategies that gave the employees a sense of ownership in how their department operated. That, in and of itself, boosted morale and allowed creative ideas to emerge, prompting innovations that improved their product.

To this day, the business continues to operate from a team effort, where management and employees are mindful and in service to each other. They are able to listen, cooperate, and make clear decisions. They have moved beyond "it'll be what it'll be" to the potential of "we can make it what we want."

Here is another example of deep listening to identify an organization's culture. The mission of the firm is: "Quality, Value, and Convenience." As I did intake individually with the management group, I heard several speak about how they were becoming "more **conscious** of **how** we work, not just **what** we do." The word "conscious" provided some interesting dialogue in terms of the principle of Consciousness. I pointed out that "conscious" and "Consciousness" are connected, and how the ability to become more aware is innate. In our discussion, we were able to establish the relevance and importance of being more aware from a clear state of mind, and how a clear mind affects the way people work. Quality, value and convenience are more apt to happen if the workforce is thinking clearly; and a clear mind allows employees to be more in service to each other and to their customers.

The statement of "**how** we work, not just **what** we do" also struck a chord in me that resonated with the principle of Thought. I could see there was a deep connection between **how** they think and **how** they work, which, if they could see the power of Thought in creating their experience, would build a bridge between their world of commerce and the world of Principle. The knowledge of the nature of Thought and how Thought works would enhance their mission, and certainly lend itself to their working together with more cohesion.

Knowledge is of little use without results or outcome. Successful business leaders know this intuitively. They know that in order for employees to perform at their highest level, the culture of the organization must offer support, encouragement and an open ear. Whenever deep, healthy feelings are present, we all have access to wisdom, common sense and creative intelligence; the Principle of Mind. When we open the connection to Mind, our personal mind is free and clear to explore new ideas, and insights abound. This leads to superior performance.

One organization that has had some education in Three Principles culture change programs found that morale improved substantially. Productivity and efficiency improved as management and employees began to see the relevance of a clear state of mind, and to work together toward that end. They began to feel better about themselves and each other. They enjoyed working together cooperatively rather than having "turf" or "them versus us" issues.

When the Board of Directors heard about the dramatic results of the culture change, they toured the facility and were heard to comment on the camaraderie and well-being they observed in the employees, at all levels. Naturally, this improvement in productivity and efficiency resulted in significantly less re-work, which enhanced the bottom line. The Board didn't really know about the Principles training that was being done in the organization, but they liked what they saw and were respectful, supportive, and offered encouragement for the change in the company's culture.

Welcome and cherish your healthy feelings. Healthy feelings are contagious. Mindfulness, gratitude, appreciation and kindness act as fuel for a clear path to efficiency, superior performance, and Principle-based leadership.

Accountability with Compassion

There are times when we struggle with a loved one; a spouse, family member, friend or colleague, and find ourselves at a loss. Separate realities come into play in a way that seems real and not illusionary. We may feel our point of view is the "right" one. Of course, the person we are struggling with also feels he or she is "right." The power of Thought brings our fretful, concerned thoughts to life. We are gripped by emotion that is not healthy, productive or conducive to bringing about solutions. How to resolve this dilemma?

There seems no easy answer when one is caught up in unhealthy thoughts and emotions. Sometimes, when certain issues have come up repeatedly over a period of time, it can be difficult to maintain perspective. We may feel we have been as patient and understanding as we can be, and now have come to the "end of our rope." This is the time most fraught with the pitfalls of ego, power and control concerns.

Yet there is another power at our fingertips, a power that offers us solace and solutions. To access this power one must have the strength of a lion and the meekness of a lamb, and the honesty to look at our role in the interaction of the relationship. No matter how real the issues are, the spiritual fact of the matter is, only a shift in consciousness will allow us clarity of mind to see creative solutions. A mind that is filled with angry, sorrowful, resentful thoughts will prevent resolution.

With a shift in consciousness comes compassion. Compassion is a power greater than ego, greater than the personal self and greater than the issue of a power struggle. With compassion comes understanding, and at the same time accountability. Compassion is imbued with selflessness coupled with a sense of purpose. With this certainty, it is possible to bring light and lightheartedness to a problem that begs for illumination.

A teacher shared the following story with me:

"I have a fifteen year old student who is considered by the system to be at-risk, although I do not see her that way. Her mother came to me very concerned, because she discovered her daughter had been exploring chat rooms on the internet, had met a boy online, and had gotten together several times with him. The girl also seemed to be withdrawing from her home and family.

"The mother was frantic, understandably, and spoke harshly to her daughter about her concerns. This action prompted rebellion on the part of the daughter, concluding with her staying out all night. When she came in the next morning, without any apparent harm, the mother was overwrought with her worries, and immediately grounded her daughter for the next month.

"As I listened to the mother telling me this story, it appeared there was little dialogue between the two. It sounded like it was more the mother telling the daughter what she expected from her in the future, and setting the parameters for her daughter's behavior.

"My heart went out to this mother because I am a mother myself, and have experienced sleepless nights fraught with worry over my own children. However, I was able to see that the way she had handled this situation was tantamount to waving a red flag in front of a bull. Setting parameters and grounding an adolescent who misbehaves is only one way of dealing with an event. There are other options.

"As I continued to listen to the mother pour her heart out to me, she began to share the constructive qualities she had seen in her daughter in times past. She was so hurt and disappointed that these qualities seemed to have disappeared. As she talked about the positive side of her daughter, her whole face changed to one of love. This stirred me, and it occurred to me to ask, 'Have you told your daughter what you just shared with me?'

"The mother was stunned momentarily, then burst into tears and said, 'No. She's been acting out so much that there hasn't been time, nor have I felt inclined to tell her about her positive qualities because they aren't in evidence right now.'

"'Your love for her is so obvious,' I replied. 'I have no doubt that if you told her this instead of focusing on her poor behavior, she would be moved by your love. When she sees and feels your love, she is more apt to trust you and talk with you than when you are trying to control her without understanding.

"'I encourage you to nourish the feeling of good-will with your daughter. When the feeling between you is healthy, you will know what to do. I feel certain that when you and your daughter focus on the love you have for each other, you will both come to a healthier solution together.'"

The teacher's story of mother and daughter touched my heart. It brought to mind those times when our children were young and misbehaving. Usually we were misbehaving too, didn't realize it, and therefore couldn't hear what our children were trying to tell us.

I remember the time, years ago, when our young son had a slight accident with my Honda Civic. He had just learned to drive and was a little nervous, and bumped into a cement barrier. A bit of damage was done that was easily taken care of, and nothing much was said.

A few weeks later, he had another accident. Once again, not much damage, but a little more was said. "After all," I thought, "two accidents in a row; he needs to be more careful." Then the third accident happened, and this one was more serious. Our son was speeding and turned the car over into a ditch. Fortunately for him and his friends in the car, no one was hurt. The car was damaged and required a good deal of repair.

At this point, my husband, Ken, and I realized that we needed to pay more attention to our son and involve him more in the discussion of accountability. Prior to this, I had assumed responsibility for the accidents, both in terms of taking care of the damage, and of not having more of a heart to heart with our son. I let him avoid responsibility and accountability.

Ken and I ended up having an open and honest discussion with our son, asking his opinion on how this situation could be handled. At first he was a bit tentative, but when he realized we were intent on listening to him with respect, he opened up and took full responsibility for his actions.

The plan he came up with was more disciplined than we would have asked for, but we saw this was meaningful for him and abided by his decision. He felt that he should not drive the car for the next month and he paid for the repairs, as well as the increase in insurance.

This was a watershed moment for the three of us, and we moved to another level of respect and understanding in our relationship. The solution was love and listening. Out of that came whatever was most appropriate for that moment in time.

Here is another example of accountability with compassion. A community project required a simple survey of the residents, prior to a Principle based leadership-training program. The project director hired several residents to conduct the survey, and gave them a briefing on how to manage the data. Since many in the community were illiterate, those hired were advised to read the questions to the residents, and draw out answers from them.

When the director received the surveys back and glanced through them to see if they were properly filled in, she noticed there were numerous forms from one surveyor that were similar, all scoring high on questions about well-being and mental health. As this was a crime-ridden, in many ways desperate area, it didn't make sense to the director that these residents' scores would present such a rosy picture. She pondered the situation, and felt a possible answer was that the staff member had answered the questions on the resident's behalf, rather than eliciting answers from them.

The director wasn't sure how to handle this situation, since the residents who were hired to conduct the survey, while briefed on the process, had never done this type of job before. Their self-esteem was not high and she didn't want to diminish their emerging sense of self-worth by questioning their newly found ability. She finally decided to just ask the surveyor what she thought about this state of affairs.

To the director's surprise, the surveyor openly stated that she had answered the questions on the residents' behalf. She wanted to show the residents in the best possible light, even though she acknowledged they were very stressed and troubled by the conditions in their community and in their families. She hadn't wanted her community to look bad in the researchers' eyes.

After more in-depth conversation, explaining the necessity for an honest evaluation that would reflect positive change as the residents completed the training program, the staff member volunteered to survey her group again, on her own time, and to let them answer the questions in their own words.

The director and surveyor had a good chuckle as they considered what the researchers might have thought had the incorrectly scored surveys been turned in. They might have assumed the residents didn't need any help at all, given their mentally healthy state. They might even have felt that the residents could have trained other communities in how to achieve this high degree of health.

As a matter of fact, this is just what happened. After the leadership training, the first year evaluation demonstrated a significant change in people's state of mind. The residents were asked to train others in their community, and in other neighborhoods.

When you trust that people have innate mental health within them and look to that resource, mental health will become evident. When we focus on poor behavior, that focal point will prompt more poor behavior. The power of love and compassion brings accountability into motion in a gentle, reliable and enduring manner. This is what our True Identity offers.

The Art of Relationships

Relationships are a wonderful gift. The gift of friendship, at its best, brings understanding from the heart, without words. Relationships offer love, companionship, humor, comfort and solace in times of need; connections that sustain the human spirit. What is the key to maintaining strong, vital relationships, whether with spouse, partner, family members, friends, or co-workers?"

Years ago, my friends changed frequently. I would have a friend for a few years, then after a period of time, the friendship seemed to peter out; not for any reason that I could see. It just seemed there wasn't the same energy or interest remaining. I must say, often times the friendship would end because of a disagreement that seemed impossible to resolve. So, I would find a new friend. Our relationship would be quite enjoyable for a time, and then that friendship would also fade away. This was the pattern of my life until I learned about the fundamental nature of experience.

Once I gained some understanding of the Three Principles, and how human beings create experience, my relationships changed. The first relationship to change was the relationship with myself. I discovered I had more within me than I had previously considered. As I began to get in touch with my True Identity, I realized I was a nicer person than I had thought.

Prior to that revelation, I had felt very unsure of myself, and would focus on my shortcomings rather than my strengths. Of course, that manner of thinking brought on even more insecure behavior. I did the same thing with my friends. Focusing on their inadequacies, rather than their strengths, led to short term relationships. I couldn't see the logic of this outcome, because I didn't know, at the time, how behavior was created. Now, it seems so obvious, it's humorous.

The difference in my life, as I began to discern my inner self, was amazing to me. I felt an emerging confidence, hopefulness, and a feeling of being at ease in my own skin. The feeling of well-being overlapped all my relationships, allowing me to naturally be nicer to everyone with whom I came in contact. There was no plan or effort on my part to be more positive. The feeling of happiness seemed to materialize in the most natural way, as if it was innate...

It made sense to me that if I had innate resources, then everyone must have access to the same resources, because at our core, we are all the same spiritual essence. I realized that we all have the gift of innate mental health, which is our default setting, our birthright.

Prior to that insight, I believed what I had learned in childhood; that people were born contaminated by original sin. Nothing was gained from this belief but grief; it evoked fear, judgment, guilt, blame and rigidity. I never imagined there was any other way to think; I had too much trepidation to even consider any other ideas on the subject.

Consequently, whenever I thought about myself, it was in a self-conscious way, an insecure way. Seldom had I contemplated my own being; seldom had I stopped to consider my life and wonder whether I could be happy. I had accepted the status quo of my existence as a given; that's just the way life was.

With fresh insight, I saw that my ***thinking*** was contaminated, not me! I realized that I was more than my thoughts. When I began to comprehend the spiritual fact that we are more than our thoughts, that we are spiritual beings, I lost my fear of change. It was as if a load of bricks had been taken off my back, and my life blossomed with lightness and a renewed vigor. I was filled with eagerness to experience life to the fullest, not simply to cope with and endure life.

My new outlook transferred to my relationships. I found, to my surprise and delight, that I felt a new understanding for my husband and children, for my family, for my old friends. They were endearing to me in a way I hadn't felt before. It was as if I was seeing them with new eyes; eyes that had less judgment, less blame, more love and forgiveness. I felt a certainty in myself, of being able to handle any challenge that might appear. With the courage of insight and the strength of conviction, I felt armed with the knowledge that everyone is a spiritual being.

The shift into healthy functioning, I found, was contagious. I perceived that this quality of health attracts and engages others. I found many new friends from all walks of life; people who were open to new thinking, who were what I consider "naturals" in their positive outlook. Even though they may not have understood the workings of the mind, they had an uplifting spirit.

Gaining an understanding of how the Three Principles create the human experience will renew and refresh all relationships. I've observed countless couples come together, and stay together, supporting each other with love and strong commitment. Often times, these couples were in dire trouble before they were introduced to the Principles. Their relationships were transformed, as they gained a deeper understanding of human interaction.

My husband, Ken and I, have been married for forty-seven years. In a way, I feel the relationship "feeds itself" because we have so much love and respect for each other. We cherish and nurture quiet times of communication. Much of the time, we continue to see each other with new eyes, because we are always evolving into new people. Ken tells me that I often still surprise him by saying or doing something unexpected, and I am delighted to say the same about him.

Seeing each other with new eyes is a marvelous antidote to straying. You have heard the old saying, "The grass is always greener on the other side of the fence"? Consider this; living in an ever-deepening acknowledgement of the Principles permits the grass to stay green in your own yard. You don't have to seek vitality or excitement with other partners when you and your partner are content, and satisfied with each other. When rocky times come around, you learn to communicate with respect, keeping each other's dignity intact. Nurture the loving, respectful feeling, and you can't go wrong. The deep feeling of love is what waters and fertilizes the relationship to keep it healthy.

To my utter enjoyment, our sense of humor has deepened. Ken and I find life much more amusing than we used to. Life isn't as serious as we previously thought. It's not that we don't have events happen which certainly could be taken seriously. It's just that we see them with clearer eyes that allow solutions to more readily appear. If one gets gripped by a certain event, usually the other is able to coach gently and help stabilize the situation.

Our love is more unconditional, more accepting of who we are, with faults and strengths equally acknowledged. We find that we can agree to disagree, and still have a respectful, loving feeling. We trust that we each will learn in our own way, and at our own pace. Still, we know we are only beginning our journey; we have much to learn, with gratitude paving our way.

This seemingly magical, yet practical, aspect of the Principles is demonstrated in many other ways. In my work, I have found that people from every walk of life are drawn to the feeling of well-being, as to a warm fire. The positive feeling lights the fire within, and movement occurs. Goodwill, unleashed and coupled with newfound understanding, allows one to make a new life that is more joyful, productive and satisfying.

When the light is turned on, we are able to see through the fog of assumptions and prejudices that cloud relationships.

We are able to find the essential core within mankind—something we may never have dreamed existed.

There have been many times when I was told you couldn't introduce the Principles to the business world, that people were more concerned with the "hard facts" of business, rather than the "soft touch" of philosophy. That has not been my experience. If the feeling of good-will is in place, I have found the business community is just like any other group. Some will resonate with this understanding, and others won't. Some will make great strides; their lives will be transformed, and they will touch countless others. People are people, no matter what position, profession or standing.

Leaders in organizations who have been educated in the Three Principles have found new ways of leading. They've invited their employees in as part of the team, and listened to them in a way they had never done before. Prior to this shift in understanding, leadership had been more by coercion, rather than by rapport and developing solid relationships. The growing camaraderie brought attention to a broader base of employees, and new leaders emerged from every level, not just management.

Deepening our understanding deepens our relationships. Strong relationships, when they are anchored in a grateful understanding of the Principles, support people and help them feel safe. Feeling safe and secure enables them to see the present with hopefulness. Being in the moment, experiencing every nuance of life, and appreciating the ability to learn from every experience…to my mind, that is why we are here. What better way to bring more harmony into our world?

Not Looking for Outcome

Why is it that sometimes the more you pursue a goal, the more elusive it becomes? Why is it that pursuing a goal can create stress and anxiety and actually prevent you from achieving it? If you don't pursue goals, does this mean you can't accomplish what you set out to do?

An interesting conversation took place recently in a group I was working with. People were discussing whether it was possible to achieve goals without stress. They were also considering whether it was feasible to do projects without expectations, trusting that things would turn out for the best. The conversation went something like this:

John: "I know that when I have expectations, I am often disappointed if things don't turn out the way I anticipated. Then I am stressed by disappointment and failure. It seems like a double edged sword."

Shirley: "I know what you mean. I have a small, home-based business that I want to expand. I've put together a comprehensive business plan, with numbers that I've projected in order to meet my financial goals. It's not working as well as I'd like. I've gone over and over the figures, tightening up and refining my projections, yet I'm not pleased with the outcome. I find myself becoming stressed about my goals."

As I was listening to the conversation, it occurred to me that I seldom look for outcomes anymore. I shared with the group that the more we trust our wisdom, the more we are taken care of. Living life with appreciation, and an understanding of the operating Principles underlying human behavior, provides a safeguard. It's not that we don't experience difficulties from time to time, but if we continue to function from wisdom, we will more likely be able to handle anything that comes our way.

This doesn't mean that I don't plan projects or have goals, but I let them unfold naturally. I do find that my goals have changed, that they are based on seeing the spiritual core in people, and engaging and drawing out that divine spark.

The other goal is to "just show up" in a healthy state of mind, wherever the location, whatever the project. In other words, I live my life, as much as I can, trusting that when my state of mind is healthy, things will unfold in the most appropriate way; often times, far beyond what I could have anticipated. This process is most enjoyable, and seems to attract people to you, as if drawn to the warmth of sunshine.

I related the following examples to the group. A realtor I know has a remarkable philosophy. He's not concerned about whether he sells houses or not! We all know that in the real estate business, the goal is selling houses, businesses, property and so on. Yet here is a man, very successful, who is not concerned about selling. He enjoys meeting interesting people from all over the world, loves to converse with them and is in service to their needs. He doesn't push them, but lets them take their own time; he will actually advise them to wait until it feels "right" to them. Consequently, his clients are relaxed with him. They are thinking more clearly, are more decisive, and the realtor sells more real estate. He's happy and his clients are happy.

The realtor tells me that when he does get stressed about a sale, he can see very quickly how it affects his business and his clients. Everything seems to be more effortful and the clients less certain. He says that learning about the Principles helped him be more sensitive to noticing this. He said it gives him more perspective, and he doesn't get as anxious. He is able to move back fairly quickly into well-being.

Here's another example. A labor relations specialist related this story to me when I asked him about his work.

"I see my job is to help people relax. It doesn't matter whether I'm dealing with union or management. People are people, and I look to the innate health in individuals, no matter what behavior is being exhibited. When people relax, they tend to respond, rather than react. They are more cooperative, with me and with each other. So that's all I do; I help people relax, and then we do whatever we need to do.

"Not everyone likes my philosophy about helping the client relax before we conduct business. They assume that I'm not serious about my work because I take the time to really listen. However, I find that negotiations move along smoothly and problems are circumvented. Ultimately, even the colleagues who are skeptical often end up curious, because things have gone so well."

Another colleague, Joyce, who was on a management negotiating committee, had a similar story to tell. No one on the committee had any education on the Three Principles, except Joyce. Her calm state of mind helped stabilize the negotiating team, so there was less yelling and more listening from each side. Each team became less entrenched in their agenda. Nothing was said about state of mind; Joyce demonstrated by example. The example of keeping calm helped people operate from a healthier place.

Joyce told me that when first asked to sit on the committee, she was nervous. She was inexperienced in this area, and wondered if she would be able to handle it. She said the only thing that came to mind was to "show up" in as healthy a state of mind as possible, and to listen. "I wasn't expecting anything because I didn't know what to expect. Not knowing what to expect left my mind free and clear, so I was able to listen more deeply, be in the moment, and be in service in a way I hadn't experienced before. It was a remarkable occurrence for me, and I saw the impact it had on the team."

As the group listened to these examples, a contemplative silence fell. Nothing was said for several minutes. Then, Shirley, the woman who had been concerned about not meeting her goals for expanding her small business, spoke up.

"What I'm hearing from these stories is that if have a shift in my level of consciousness, I will relax and enjoy my business more. I'll worry less about projections so I may do better. It's certainly worth a try. I'm not happy now with my stressful feelings, so I've got nothing to lose. I'll let you know how it works out."

The group erupted into spontaneous laughter at her innocent admission about not being happy with her stress. It struck the group as amusing; suddenly her face creased into a wide smile as she caught the contagious humor. I knew she had already deepened her understanding; I knew she had heard something very important to her.

Shirley called me not long after our group meeting. She told me that when she returned to her business, there were many calls inquiring about her product. "I've never been so busy. I've sold more in one week than I had in the previous month. I don't know if our discussion and my insight had anything to do with this, but I'm grateful for the increased business. It has taught me a lesson. Stress doesn't help me to achieve my goals. My goals are best achieved when I relax and enjoy my work. So now, my goal is to enjoy my work! It doesn't really feel like a goal; more like a way of life."

I appreciated Shirley's shift in perspective. Even though she hadn't yet connected her increased business to her healthier state of mind, I felt it was only a matter of time. The fact that she was grateful was an indication of her connection to deeper feelings. Deeper feelings are the route to more understanding, and a healthier quality of life.

As a consumer myself, I know when I meet someone in a place of business, whether a restaurant, corporate office, warehouse, or whatever the business may be, and he or she is relaxed and at ease, I find myself more relaxed, and enjoying the conversation.

Certainly, plans and projections are important, and necessary when appropriate. Just remember to enjoy them!

Attachment to Well-Being

Can your concern for another get in the way of their finding their own wisdom? When this question started to tickle my consciousness, I was thinking in terms of being emotionally involved in someone else's well-being.

Let me explain by offering you this scenario. John's cousin, Ben, had been struggling mentally for some time. Ben was divorced, and had problems with his fourteen year old son, who had left home to live with his mother. Over the past year, Ben had focused on what he perceived to be his failure as a parent. He was experiencing stressful thoughts of guilt, blame, and resentment.

From time to time, Ben would call John, seeking counsel. John did his best to point Ben back to his own innate wisdom. At the same time, John reinforced the positive aspects he saw in Ben's parenting. To John's surprise, this did not go over well with his cousin. Rather than appreciating his positive comments, Ben seemed upset by them.

This turn of events gave John pause. Clearly, in an unhealthy state of mind, Ben couldn't conceive that he had been a good parent at all. If he had been a good parent, he felt his son wouldn't have left home. He couldn't conceive that his son may have left home to be with his mom for any other reason. Consequently, he told his cousin that what he was saying did not have merit. It had no place in his world, because his world looked very different than the one to which John was pointing.

John's concern for Ben's well-being led him to continue to try and help him, in subtle ways. He did this by calling occasionally, being in the moment, and letting the conversation unfold. Still, even in these conversations, John felt gripped by Ben's low moods. Although he tried not to let it get him down, inevitably he would be drawn into feeling sorry for Ben. John knew that feeling sorry for someone is a poor substitute for compassion. He knew that when he was in the "sorry mode," his own state of mind was negatively affected. John had experienced compassion before as a non-judgmental, loving feeling. But at this point, non-judgment was eluding him. He was also beginning to get impatient with his cousin's "poor me" attitude.

As time went on, there was a shift in John's consciousness. The light went on in his head when he realized that he was getting involved in his cousin's thinking, rather than trusting Ben's wisdom. It dawned on him that in his "helping" he was innocently contributing to Ben's struggle. Because Ben didn't like the positive aspect of John's coaching, it added another layer to his resistance, thereby keeping him even further away from his own insights.

He was needlessly taking on the responsibility of trying to "fix" someone. With the best intentions, John was getting in the way of Ben finding his inner wisdom, in his own way, and at his own pace.

This insight helped John see that just ***being*** with Ben, and enjoying life, had more value than anything he could say. Seeing the value of ***being*** rather than ***doing*** brought John great relief and peace of mind. His wisdom shone as a beacon, illuminating the way for those who chose to pay attention.

Our True Identity is buoyant, and automatically bounces back, if we don't continue to cover it by layers of personal thinking. If we hold our negative thoughts in our mind, we keep ourselves prisoners of our thinking. While we're focused on ***trying*** to stay in a good mood, or to shift others in that direction, we have moved into ***doing*** rather than ***being***.

To see moods as an ordinary process in life offers much relief and neutrality. It releases you from the struggle of trying to maintain a good mood. You become less attached to your well-being because you are discovering your inner divine core. You know your wisdom will re-emerge.

Surface water can be disturbed by ripples and eddies; yet under the ripples, the water is calm. In like manner, your surface thinking, another way of saying personal thinking, can be rippled. Underneath the ripples, divine wisdom is calm, a foundation of spiritual strength.

Seeing moods simply as a part of learning brings a feeling of gratitude. This deep feeling will replace whatever stressful thoughts you may have been ruminating on before. You will experience a deeper level of knowing; you will have found another piece to the puzzle and mystery of life.

It continues to amaze me that we often seem to learn the same thing over and over again, as we move to deeper levels of understanding. When this happens, the information appears fresh and insightful. Confusion falls away, and what once seemed subtle now becomes clear.

SEEING Beyond Personal Identity

Considering a human being simply as a personality is a barrier to seeing that person's True Identity. It prevents us from seeing the individual as a unique spiritual being, on the same journey that all of us travel. When we see the outer garment of the soul, and take the garment as the total package, we miss out on the essence of the individual.

Being aware of this spiritual fact offers a neutral perspective that allows clearer thinking, and the ability to take things less personally. Taking circumstances personally can leave us feeling immobilized by uncertainty, rendered helpless by indecision, and by situations that we, ourselves have created. It's not a pleasant place to live. I've visited there many times and am grateful not to linger.

Think how freeing it is when we trust that each soul has the innate ability to ***see***, and to make life what he or she wants. We don't need to take responsibility for others' happiness. Interestingly, this outlook affords more impact when we realize that we can't "fix" anyone; we can only offer assistance, and respect whether the assistance is rejected or accepted.

Dwelling on what is wrong can lead to conclusions based on false assumptions, creating a repetitious cycle of blame, guilt, and resentment. Knowledge and experience does not make you immune from struggle; but wisdom does offer respite, and the ability to move ahead without carting the past with you.

Seeing beyond personal identity to your own True Identity offers a neutral playground. You are free and open to others' ideas and thoughts. You listen beyond the word to what is truly being said. Uncovering your True Identity leads to seeing beyond affectations, and straight into the heart and soul of an individual.

A client, Peter, shared this story with me. "My ex-wife left me a message the other day to call her. When I returned her call, I found she was upset because her alimony check was late. She thought I was playing games with her, and had sent it late deliberately. This wasn't the case at all. I had mailed it, but evidently it got lost in the mail. I know, I know! You've heard this line before, but it is true.

"I listened to her for a moment, and then jumped in with my defense. She didn't let me get a word in edgewise. She hammered at me verbally, and before I knew it, I was in the fray with her. I was definitely taking the situation personally. I ended the conversation by telling her I would look into it and courier another check, canceling the lost one.

"I don't know what to make of this, Elsie. I thought I had enough on the ball not to get so upset with her again. Why does this happen? Why did I react again so quickly, rather than listen to her and hear her out?"

Had Peter ***seen*** beyond his ex-wife's personal identity and viewed her as a spiritual being, he would have had an entirely different conversation with her. When an individual lashes out, you have the choice of seeing only the negative behavior/personality, or seeing a spiritual being, who is temporarily caught up in his or her own insecure thoughts.

When you are seeing the personal identity, you react. When you see the True Identity, you respond. When you react, chances are the conversation is over before it begins. When you respond, the conversation holds promise and understanding. From this point of discernment, the difference between the two interactions makes perfect sense.

Life, being a contact sport, provides us with countless opportunities to "walk our talk." Usually, just when we think we're living in harmony with the world around us, another opportunity tests our mettle to see what we've learned so far. It's good to stretch our mind beyond what we think we know; even though sometimes we may think, "I'm stretched enough!"

Despite the traditional belief that confusion is not a good thing, confusion and bewilderment can be reminders that there is always more to learn. These two factors can aerate the mind and let new thoughts in, allowing for growth and deeper mental health. It is similar to when you aerate the lawn, then fertilize and water. Soon the lawn is green and healthy.

A wise friend made this statement the other day. "You either operate from love or from fear." Those words and the love behind them were a much-needed source of strength for me at that moment in time. I was in a morose mood that day. A dear friend had neglected to send me a birthday card, or to call and wish me a happy birthday. This individual had never forgotten before. My relationship with my friend had been going through some changes, and in my insecurity, my feelings were hurt. I took the absence of the card and call personally.

On the other hand, my mother-in-law also neglected to send a card or call on my birthday. This occurrence wasn't an issue for me, and didn't bother me at all. I saw beyond her personal identity as my mother-in-law to her spiritual essence. I understood she was aging and forgetful, so I continued to operate from love. Consequently, my feelings weren't hurt, and I didn't take it personally. Yet in the case of my close friend, it took a shift in perspective to see beyond my expectations. Insight took me beyond his personal identity to see his spiritual core, to see his innocence. Suffice to say, this understanding state of mind is a much nicer place to live.

Another humorous example of ***seeing*** beyond identity and beliefs is of observing Ken, my husband, in a different light. Ken was building a new master bathroom in our home. We were at the stage of choosing paint. After I selected a color that Ken painted on two walls, I felt that the color wasn't quite right with the tiles in the shower or the bathtub surround. Ken showed great forbearance, and we agreed that I would pick up some other paint charts and bring them home for Ken to view.

While at the paint store, I solicited the advice of the color consultant, having brought a sample of the tiles we were using. With her help, I selected some paint charts to take home. One chart had bold russet tones that I didn't think Ken would go for, and mentioned this to the consultant. She suggested I take them anyway and see what he would say. I left with my choice of more neutral tones of toffee cream that I felt he would prefer. I was leaning toward the neutral tones myself but also had in hand the bold russet chart. I presented them to Ken, certain that he would choose the softer tones.

To my total surprise he selected the bold russet shade! I couldn't believe it! You think you know someone's taste after living together for forty-seven years. It was a great opportunity to see beyond my perception of Ken's relaxed, calm identity to a "colorful" daring persona.

At first I couldn't envision the rich russet paint on the walls but did consider both colors in different lights in the bathroom to see what looked best. Still, I was stuck in the belief that the more neutral tones would be softer and more relaxing. Ken liked the pizzazz and warmth of the bold color. To his credit, he didn't push me; he just let me come to it on my own. Gradually, I saw beyond my usual habits, and noticed that the rich tones would bring life to the bathroom, given that we had neutral tones in there already.

The ability to ***see*** beyond personal identity and belief works in every facet of your life. Not just with philosophic or esoteric ideas but in the most practical, mundane, everyday events of life. That's the beauty of human beings discovering their True Identity; having access to wisdom that is all encompassing.

Understanding the Nature of Change

Have you ever been apprehensive about events and circumstances changing in your life? Have you ever been moved to consider altering your life, and then vacillated because you were uncertain, or reluctant to take that first step? Has change ever been thrust upon you, and you have resented it and fought tooth and nail to resist the move? If so, then perhaps this chapter will be of interest to you.

I'm sure we all agree that no one is immune to change. It seems the nature of life to be constantly changing; to remain static goes against the laws of the universe. In order to learn and grow, it makes sense that human beings are offered opportunities to transform, either freely, or with resistance. Even when things happen that appear to serve no purpose; even in times of unexpected tragedy or upheaval, a question to ask ourselves is: What can be learned from this? Is there a rationale beyond our comprehension?

Knowing that we have the power to create our experience in life is fundamental in understanding and moving gracefully with the flow of change. When people don't understand the role of thought in generating feelings and emotions, we become victims of change rather than victors. When we invite fear into our world, we can be tossed and buffeted by the currents of life. We emerge bedraggled and defeated, hesitant to take a chance because we fear change; because we fear failure. Yet, what is change or failure but thought?

Consider someone contemplating leaving a job, in order to pursue a dream of doing something more enjoyable. That person could become caught up in worrying about all the things that might go wrong. After all, the bills still need to be paid, and health insurance is a primary concern. Children in college still need to be supported, and there is a certain life style to be maintained.

Yes, all of these items require thoughtful evaluation and consideration; however, we don't want to dwell on them to the point of becoming entrenched. Our heads can become filled with noise when, in reality, we long for silence and solitude to cultivate life's most precious gift, wisdom.

When our minds are quiet, we can ***see*** what needs to be done to help our dreams become reality. ***Seeing*** is wisdom unfolding. Worrying is personal thinking taking over your life, to the exclusion of wisdom.

When change happens, it can be an opportunity to move ahead, to respond to an inner quest for deeper satisfaction in life. Recognizing this will help calm your thinking, providing more space in your mind for solutions to occur; for wisdom to emerge to guide your actions. Rather than relying solely on your personal thinking to lead you, realize and utilize the endowment of innate wisdom that we all are gifted with, another way of talking about our soul.

Change in itself is a neutral process, although I know it doesn't usually look that way. In reality, it is only our thinking makes it positive or negative. In the midst of transition, there is learning and spiritual growth to be gained. It is so helpful to ***know*** and trust that your soul is your best friend. Your soul offers constant solace to you in a way that no one else can. Be still, and ***know*** that your soul is a part of Divine Mind. As such, it has infinite power to comfort and guide.

Here is a story that may broaden the scope of seeing wisdom and change work together as a joint venture. In 1996, I was offered the opportunity of moving to Los Angeles from Tampa. There were several inner city Principle-based community projects on the go, and the manager of these projects wanted some assistance from me. I wasn't interested in moving there, but agreed to be a consultant for programs that were being initiated in various parts of Los Angeles County.

Twice more, I was offered the opportunity to move to Los Angeles to work there. Ken and I discussed this at length, but I couldn't conceive of living in that huge city, especially considering all the crime related stories I had heard. Finally, I was invited to a staff meeting at the California School of Professional Psychology (CSPP) where a Principle-based Institute had been started.

I accepted the invitation. When I arrived, I discovered I was the only non-staff person at the meeting. The head of the department took me to lunch and offered me a position with CSPP. He explained that they were starting a new three-year project for Volunteers of America (VOA). He said they would like me to work with them, designing and delivering the training for the multitude of programs that VOA offered, and more specifically for the homeless shelter staff. VOA was in the process of planning and building a new, innovative Homeless Shelter in skid row, Los Angeles.

I met the President of VOA and several of the staff. I read the grant that VOA had drafted outlining the program, and I was taken with the "feeling" of the proposal. In the grant, VOA talked about the homeless population as their "guests." That phrase touched my heart. I thought to myself, "If they see their clients as their guests, then there is something special going on here. I want to work with these people."

For the first time, I felt drawn to move to Los Angeles and to accept the position I was being offered. However, I was sure Ken would never go for it, as he had voiced objections when we had discussed the possibility before. To my utter and complete surprise, when I called him from Los Angeles to ask him his opinion, he barely paused before responding, "Yes, I think you should seriously consider this offer. I'm also ready for a change."

Within a month, Ken tendered his notice at work, and listed and sold our home. He moved into a motel while waiting for me to return from my work in Los Angeles. Things were moving along very smoothly, although I did have moments of trepidation about finding a home in LA, and many other details that were on my mind. Overall, I felt elated, and eager to settle into our new surroundings, whatever they might be.

One last program, at a Women's College in Virginia, had to be completed before I returned home to Florida. I flew there from Los Angeles. The first day of training went very well and I felt that I had the group on board.

That night, I got a call from the manager of the programs that I was to be helping with, telling me that he had resigned from CSPP. He explained his rationale for doing this. I understood his position and agreed with his stand. I felt like a split personality. While I understood why he resigned, I still felt as if the rug had been pulled out from under me. Because of his resignation, my position was no longer valid at CSPP so I was without a job. Frankly, had my colleague been in the room with me at that point in time, I probably would have gone up one side of him and down the other. My wisdom was hidden behind a cloud of very personal thinking.

What to do now? Ken, having given up his career, was waiting for me in a motel in Tampa. Upon my return, we planned to drive to Los Angeles together. Now we had nothing to go to; no job, and a beautiful condominium in Long Beach that we couldn't afford. In the midst of this dilemma, I'm in Virginia, conducting a program at the Women's College, wanting to be at my best and in a clear state of mind so I can be of service to my clients.

I called Ken and briefly explained the situation. He listened attentively, saying little. We agreed to leave any decisions until I arrived home.

I tossed and turned that night, not knowing what the future held. The next morning, when I met with our group, a state of calm came over me. I was in service to the team. I gained respite from my own concerns. I realized that knowledge is of little use without wisdom, and that wisdom is spiritual in nature. It came to me that true spirituality always includes service to others and that you also end up as a beneficiary.

When I arrived home, Ken was very supportive and committed to moving to Los Angeles, regardless of the outcome. He felt we were being drawn there for a reason and should follow our hearts. Without any more hesitation, we headed across country to California. Our trip out there was wonderful. We had time with each other and time to enjoy the moment, without concern for the future. We didn't ***try*** to be in the moment; we just ***were***.

After arriving at our new home and settling in, I got together with my colleague and had an extremely productive meeting. We decided to become business partners and start our own company. VOA let us know that they wanted us to continue on their project. We were also asked by CSPP to manage one other community program. These two projects provided us with initial financial resources to support our two families.

Most importantly, although my business partner and I still had moments of insecurity about whether other projects would come our way and whether we would be able to make it, there was an underlying sense that things would work out. There was also the feeling that we were meant to be working together, and that we would learn much from each other. It was with a renewed sense of certainty and enthusiasm that we began our programs with VOA. Soon, other projects came our way.

The move to Los Angeles was a turning point for Ken and me. We realized how much wisdom prepares us for life, if we let it. Understanding that the nature of change is related to Thought, and by how we view the circumstances presented to us, makes an enormous difference, regardless of what the change looks like initially; enjoyable, or dreadful. Understanding gives you a wider perspective with which to view the many options you have. Nothing is written in stone.

You may be in a new position at work, with a new boss and a new mandate for your department. Perhaps the boss's new vision and values for the department are not in alignment with your current understanding. Could this be Divine Mind's way of broadening your perspective? Could this be an opportunity afforded you to see beyond behavior to the essence of the situation? Are you operating from security or insecurity? Are you operating from love or fear? It's all in the way we think about things that determines whether we move ahead.

There is no rush to make change. Wisdom and free will work hand in hand, allowing humans to grow at their own pace and in their own time. ***Knowing*** that we can go at our own pace makes a huge difference. ***Knowing*** that wisdom dispenses solutions to our concerns paves the way for acceptance, acceptance that offers understanding.

Your True Self will not let you forget that transition is waiting in the wings for you. You can rest easy until you accept the mandate for change. Move into the next phase of your life, knowing the process is a gentle one, if we allow it to be. Embrace change, ***knowing*** it is Divine Mind's way of uncovering our wisdom. Wisdom is the result of our soul expanding into its rightful purpose.

The Value of Positive Feelings

The infinite value of mentally healthy feelings is one of the first things we learn as we discover the three spiritual principles of Mind, Consciousness and Thought. Feelings are a gentle guide pointing the way to well-being. Feelings also let us know when our thinking is not healthy; when we are caught up in a mire of personal distraction.

Sometimes, when our emotions are anxiety driven, and we are filled with worry, concern, anger, and resentment, the path doesn't seem so gentle. The gift of wisdom, of realizing that we are the thinker of our thoughts, and that thoughts create feelings, gives us a wealth of protection from taking the full brunt of unhealthy emotions. Wisdom provides perspective with which to view our outlook in a neutral, unattached manner. Wisdom lets us know that as our thoughts change, so do our feelings. The more perspective we have, the quicker we rebound to our healthy state of mind.

We realize not to make an issue of things when we are caught up in unhealthy thinking. We learn that it is wiser to calm down and regain a better viewpoint. We learn it is not wise to quit our job, decide to move to another country, ask the boss for a raise, or have a heart to heart with a colleague or family member when we are feeling less than emotionally stable.

You may question this and say, "If I wait to do these things until I'm feeling good, I may be waiting till hell freezes over." So be it. The old cliché, ***patience is a virtue***, rings very true at this point. Nothing is gained by feeling compelled to move ahead when you sense a barrier in place. Better to follow your inner common sense, and wait until healthy functioning is restored, than to risk additional strife.

The moment you honestly check your own intention about what you want to say, and why you want to say it, is the moment you are ready to progress. What I mean by that is: if your intention is to make a point, to be "right" about something, then you are off track. The issue is not to be "right." A healthy state of mind, which provides a wider vision, is the issue. Honesty opens the door to healthy emotions and healthy listening; these give you invaluable information, guiding you to solutions.

One of the greatest benefits of recognizing and embracing positive feelings is the ability to communicate more effectively on sensitive topics with family, friends, colleagues—with everyone. When we're feeling open and flexible, filled with good will, rapport is easy and natural to establish. Rapport happens automatically. There is no mistaking the genuine affection of heart-felt feelings being expressed. It draws people in like the feeling of getting cozy in front of a fireplace, warming body and soul.

Why then, do we sometimes not realize that a positive feeling state provides practical solutions to present day dilemmas? Perhaps when you read the following example, you will come up with your own answer.

A client called me on the phone, feeling quite depressed. She tells me that she experiences wonderful feelings of well-being and gains insights when she is being counseled by a Principle-based practitioner. She experiences the same deep feelings when she attends a Three Principles conference.

"I feel so calm and peaceful when I leave the conference or finish my coaching session," she tells me. "When I go home to my family, I'm not bothered by their typical, pessimistic behavior as much as I usually am. I see their behavior as an innocent expression of their thinking and I don't take it personally. But in a couple of weeks, their actions start to get to me again. I find myself feeling miserable and it seems as if nothing has changed. I just can't seem to sustain my good feelings. It's very disheartening. What's wrong with me?"

Her cry for help tugged at my heartstrings, and as we shared a quiet moment together, a thought came to mind. "There's nothing wrong with you," I assured her, "Welcome to the club! We all go through times when we are not living in a mentally healthy state, even when we know better. That's just the game of life. However, one of the gifts of wisdom and insight is the ability to look at our life from time to time and ***see*** how we can do better. ***See*** how we can do better, without judgment against ourselves or our family." Again, I listened to the silence over the phone for a moment; then asked a question.

"When you're feeling in a positive state, do you take the opportunity to have a dialogue with your family about what you see in your domestic relationships?"

"No, I don't," she responded after a lengthy pause. "It seems to me that as long as my mood is healthy, that should be enough to create balance and harmony in our family."

"Yes, of course, your healthy mood is extremely important to understanding and sustaining family relationships. Tell me this; in your healthy state of mind, did the thought of talking to your family occur to you?"

"Well, it's interesting that you ask that question, Elsie. When I think back, I did have a niggling feeling that this would be a good time to talk with them, but I didn't. I actually thought it was my personal thinking prompting me to take action. I wasn't sure what to do, so I did nothing."

"It's understandable. Old habits creep in, and before you know it you're engaged in old behavior. Only this time, you're more aware that something is off kilter. That means you've had a shift in consciousness. You are less gripped by your old habits. This is significant, and something to be grateful for. Our consciousness is always aware; sometimes we just don't listen!"

"Are you saying that when I am in a good mood I should "do" or "make" something happen; that I should force a conversation? That sounds like ego."

"No, I don't mean that at all. It's hard to describe. When you're in a positive state, wisdom guides you. You will find yourself spontaneously ***doing*** without doing. What to do comes naturally, without thinking about it. I know that doesn't make sense. It is something that you need to experience.

"A wise friend told me that trying to describe how feelings work is like trying to describe how to ride a bicycle. It's impossible. You have the experience of riding a bike, and then you know how. In the same way, you have positive feelings, and insights occur to you. Then you know how to live life with more ease. The best you can do is encourage one to ride and support their effort. In the case of feelings, pay more attention to what wisdom is trying to tell you.

"You mentioned that you had a niggling feeling that you should talk with your family and you ignored it. Now that you realize wisdom was tickling you, the next time insight knocks on your door, you will be more receptive. You won't make good judgment wait on the doorstep as long. You will recognize the difference between the feeling of personal thinking and wisdom."

Another thought came to mind and I asked my client, "What did you feel like when the thought occurred to you to talk to your family?"

She considered my question for a moment and then declared, "I felt good and it seemed the obvious thing to do. Then I started to second guess myself, and before I knew it I was feeling uncertain. I didn't do anything."

"Sometimes when we get a message from wisdom," I mused, "and don't follow through, we feel indecisive. Then we blame our personal thinking. At that point, it is true. Our personal thinking is covering up what wisdom is trying to tell us. There are no hard and fast rules with this process.

You extend yourself, follow your feelings, and learn from your experiences.

"A shift in your level of consciousness, such as you have had, will provide more sustainability to a positive feeling state. You will find yourself and your family able to communicate with each other, with openness and curiosity, without stress."

A month later, my client called me again. Her tone was jubilant and affectionate. "Elsie, you won't believe what happened! Since our last talk, I've been seeing so much more. I've been paying more attention to my own wisdom. During dinner one evening with my family, the conversation somehow turned serious, but in a nice manner.

"We talked candidly, in a way we've not done before. The kids gradually opened up and told us more about what they were doing in school, and what they were concerned about. My husband and I listened without interrupting them. The children really seemed to appreciate it. We didn't offer advice like we normally would. Rather we asked them what they thought, and we were impressed with what they said. All we did was encourage them to follow their wisdom. The kids intuitively knew what to do; they just needed someone to listen and encourage them to follow their own counsel.

"I think the shift in our family dynamics started when I had a heart-to-heart with my husband. I told him how much I appreciate what he does for the family, and around the house. The children overheard us talking. From that point on, there was more closeness between my husband and me, and I found even more to appreciate. It's like gratitude feeds itself and expands into more enjoyment," she marveled.

"Prior to that, I was often on his case about what he ***wasn't*** doing, rather than appreciating what he ***was*** doing. That was one of the insights I had, and it worked! From now on, I am going to pay even more attention to my wisdom," she declared adamantly, concluding our talk with laughter.

This example can be transposed to any relationship, whether with business clients, friends, or colleagues. Look and ***see*** what your feelings are trying to tell you. Are you letting wisdom work for you? Are there areas in your life that would benefit by paying more attention to when wisdom is tickling you? Are you keeping wisdom on the doorstep, or inviting wisdom in to stay?

Mental Health or Mental Hurt?

Have you noticed how easy it can be to pick at the "mental hurt" when ego is involved? Mental hurt is the negative thought (or thoughts) we bring up in our minds, over and over again.

Perhaps the boss has forgotten to express appreciation to you for completing a difficult assignment. Maybe a co-worker has accepted credit and accolades of the department, for your innovative and successful idea. It could be that your sixteen year old left out some pertinent information about an unchaperoned party she attended; or your best friend failed to invite you to a dinner party, for some unknown reason, and your feelings were hurt.

Isn't it intriguing to see how mental upset changes to understanding, as you experience an upward shift in your level of consciousness? To be the observer of your own range of emotions is an endless and fascinating journey; a journey to be undertaken with deep appreciation of the role of Thought in creating feelings and emotions.

Let me tell you a story. Donald is a bright young man, who has been working with a high tech company since he graduated from college. During five years with this organization, he came up with a creative and successful computerized system that became the model for the department, and then for the whole business. Naturally, he was asked to teach others the new technology. As management took notice of his ability to lead and coach employees, he acquired a reputation as an up and coming new visionary leader in the company. Donald loved his work and continued to refine and update the program he designed. He trained others to take over more of the teaching aspects, as his time became more valuable meeting with other key leaders in the company, strategizing the future of the corporation, and utilizing the advanced computer technology.

As time went on, glitches started to develop in the computer program, but Donald was too busy to pay much attention and delegated it to his staff. His main interest now was working with the executive team. He felt his staff was quite competent in dealing with whatever was wrong with the system.

Soon a young woman, new to the company, and with a degree in computer engineering, devised a brilliant, innovative system that replaced the old program. In short order, she was sitting in on the executive team meetings, explaining how the new system was better suited for the advanced technology they needed to expand the company's retail sales tracking method.

Donald was not sure what to make of this. Things had changed so quickly that he felt he hadn't had time to adjust, and he was feeling competitive with his new colleague. He was not used to sharing the spotlight, and felt his experience was not being recognized. The more Donald thought this way, the worse he felt. Yet he couldn't seem to get out of the cycle of hurtful thoughts. Every time he thought about all he had done for the company, and how he was feeling pushed aside, he would add more hurt to his mental state.

Donald began to focus on what was wrong with his new colleague's program. He spent hours poking holes in the system and admittedly, found a few. Gleefully, he went to his boss and told him the new system wasn't as good as they thought, and they would be better to keep the old system in place. Donald said that he would work on the old system to improve it. Donald's boss suggested that Donald work with his colleague and integrate a system that would utilize the best aspects of both programs. Donald agreed with his boss, as he really had no choice; but every chance he got, he sabotaged his co-worker's efforts.

Donald was experiencing a great deal of stress, and began missing work. When he was at work, he was distracted and his job performance was poor. His sense of humor was at an all-time low, and he just couldn't seem to find anything positive to say. Everything was a problem, and his conversation was peppered with complaints. Finally, his boss sent him to the employee assistance program where he met with a counselor.

"Good afternoon, Donald. I'm Anna Baylor. I'm happy to meet you." Anna chatted with Donald for a few minutes; then, as she saw he was not into social chit chat and was fidgeting with his tie, she calmly asked, "How can I help you?"

Donald hesitated momentarily, not meeting her eyes, and then stated, "Well, my boss sent me here so I guess he thinks there is something wrong with me."

"Is there something bothering you, Donald?"

"Not really. It's just that I've spent the last five years of my life devoting myself to the company, developing a great computer program that now the company says is no good." He paused, then added, "Actually, I should say that a new staff member says the program is lacking," Donald fumed with indignation. "How dare she say that!"

"What do you think, Donald?"

"I can see that there are some glitches in the old system, but given time I know I can iron them out. However, my boss wants me to work with the new kid on the block to integrate my system with hers.

"Imagine that," he said bitterly. "I've been with the company five years, and this newcomer comes along with her new program and gets all the credit." He smiled craftily, "But I've got her number. She's not as clever as she thinks, and there are problems with her design."

Anna let Donald talk for a time until finally he paused; then she spoke, "You strike me as a very smart man, Donald, and I can see this situation has been difficult for you. Are you interested in learning about another way of perceiving this event, which will let you see beyond the behavior to the core element of the situation?"

Donald didn't say anything for a time and there was a quiet that filled the room. Reluctantly, he agreed. "I'll give it a try. I've never been to counseling before. I've never felt I had to have my head examined, but I don't feel I've got any choice."

"You've always got a choice, Donald. We won't be able to work together successfully unless you feel there is something you can get out of this session. I understand that you have taught others how to use the computer system you designed, right?"

"Right."

"What happens if the people you are educating aren't into learning?"

"They don't get it. They're very difficult to teach."

"So what's your answer? Are you interested in learning something new?"

"I get your point. Right, let's do it. This is confidential, isn't it? I wouldn't want what I tell you to get back to the boss."

"Absolutely. Whatever you have to say is between you and me," Anna reassured him.

Anna proceeded to teach him the basics of the principles of Mind, Consciousness, and Thought. She explained that there is a formless energy operating behind human behavior. When humans become aware of this inner spiritual process, they naturally create healthier behavior. She went on to say that the capacity to understand this core process is innate within every human being. It is just a matter of realizing this, and putting the knowledge to good use.

"Whatever you put into the human system is what you get out of it," Anna went on. "If you put in angry, resentful thoughts, then you get angry and resentful feelings. Input equals output."

"Now you're talking computer talk," Donald said. "That makes sense to me. But what do you do in a case like mine when the new kid on the block is deliberately out to get me?"

"Is she really? Or is it just that you ***think*** she is? And even if she is out to get you, is the way you are currently handling the event working for you?"

"No, I see what you're saying. It's not working or I wouldn't be so stressed."

"That's right, Donald. That's an excellent point. Now listen to this, it's very important. If you ***see*** the connection between your thoughts and the stress you are feeling, you will ***see*** that the way you are thinking is what creates your stress. If you relax, stop focusing on your negative thoughts, and stop picking at the mental hurt, your innate wisdom will have a chance to surface. You will have more understanding of the situation and how to handle it.

"Chances are that your new colleague is eager to work with you, given that you have more experience with the company and their needs. Why don't you give her a chance and see how she responds? And remember this, no matter how she responds; it's your response that is most important. If you maintain your healthy state of mind, you will clearly ***see*** what to do."

"Okay, I'm with you. I don't quite get all of what you've said, Anna, but much of it makes sense to me, especially the part about 'input equals output.' I've never thought about it that way before. And I've never realized that there is an operating system behind the human experience. It's quite scientific; in a way, human beings are like a computer system," Donald concluded. They arranged another session in two weeks' time. Anna gave him some of Sydney Banks' books and DVD's to review later, and then sent him on his way. He was in much better spirits than when he had arrived.

When Donald showed up at the office for the next scheduled appointment, Anna could see at once that he was distressed. Without preamble, Donald began, "You said in our last session that our thoughts create our emotions, right?"

"Yes," Anna agreed.

"Well, I've tried my best to control my thoughts, and to watch my input, but it's not working. I did experience a momentary feeling of relief after talking with you the first time, but since then, my stress seems even worse. I'm more conscious of my negative thinking and feelings. It's been hell. When I voice my opinion to my colleague about how the programs should be integrated, she doesn't listen at all. She is stubborn, and unwilling to cooperate." Donald tried to recover his composure, but clearly he was very upset.

"First of all," Anna said, "believe it or not, it's a good thing that you are more aware of your negative thoughts and emotions. Your heightened awareness means that your consciousness is awake, and helping you to realize that you're using the power of Thought against yourself. This knowledge will ultimately reduce the intensity of your emotions and eliminate your stress.

"Secondly; please understand the process is not about controlling thought. It's about ***realizing*** that you are the thinker. Realizing this allows you to be more an observer of behavior, yours and others, without becoming attached to the behavior. You will experience a more neutral stance of ***seeing*** without judging. Do you comprehend how this would enable you to ***see*** with more clarity, without judgment and stress obscuring the picture?"

"Easier said than done," Donald replied in a frustrated tone. "Aren't I entitled to an opinion, to my own thoughts?"

"Of course you are. No one can take that away from you. No one said anything about giving up your thoughts or opinions. A wise man once told me that negative thoughts can be like weeds in your mind, and will drag you down. This is where your free will comes into play, where you have a choice on what thoughts to entertain. The only question I have for you to reflect on is this: When you're in a low mood, do your thoughts and opinions serve you well?"

After some consideration, Donald responded rather sheepishly, "Certainly not the negative thoughts, or my negative opinions, either. It's just so hard to keep the focus on the positive; I feel I'm fighting a losing battle."

"Just relax, Donald, and don't take your thoughts so seriously. Take a mental vacation, and things will look brighter to you. A tip for you is this. If you're going to pick a thought to focus on, pick gratitude and appreciation."

"Gratitude?" he exclaimed. "You must be joking. Now I'm really confused. Gratitude for what; that I may be losing my job?"

Anna sat quietly, but her eyes sparkled with mischief. "Now here is a prime example of what thoughts to focus on. When you made that statement right now, what did it feel like?"

"Not great," Donald snapped.

"You mentioned when we first started our conversation today, that after our first session you did experience some mental relief from the stress you were experiencing. Let's look at that for a moment. Tell me how that happened? How did you experience relief from your negative emotions?"

Donald leaned back onto the sofa and crossed his legs. "I don't really know. I wasn't thinking of anything in particular. As I recall, I was just enjoying not feeling miserable for the first time in a long while."

"And when did you notice your stress come back?"

Again, Donald thought for a moment, and then sat forward, his elbows resting on his knees. "The stress probably came back when I started to get grief from that snippy woman who is trying to take my job." At the look on Anna's face, Donald caught himself and said, "Okay, okay, I get the message. It's got nothing to do with my co-worker, does it?" He chuckled ruefully, "There's no getting away from it. It does appear to be my thinking that is creating my stress. It's just so hard to move away from those thoughts. In one of the DVD's you gave me, I heard Sydney Banks talk about "habits of thought" and that really struck me. I guess that's what I'm experiencing, isn't it? Habits of thought," he mused.

"You've answered your own question, Donald. Good for you. The awareness that you are the thinker of the thoughts is something to feel grateful for. The insights you are getting will enhance your life and move you from feeling dissatisfied into feeling contentment. Gratitude and appreciation contribute to the sustainability of mental health. The fact that you experienced relief from stress is evidence that you have innate health within you; why not live there more of the time? All you do is let your innate wisdom bubble up inside of you. How much easier can it get?"

"So you're saying that it's my choice. I can have mental health or mental hurt? Is that right?"

"You've got it! Enjoy it!"

Good Energy

Majestic cedar boughs were decorated by nature with a light dusting of snow. Fir trees stood tall and proud, as if they understood how beautiful they looked, covered with the first snowfall of the season. Ken and I gazed out our front room window, drinking in the scene of winter wonderland, warming our hands around cups of coffee. After we admired our fill of nature, we turned back to sit in front of the fire-place, enjoying the peace and quiet of our home; the only sound was the occasional crackle of the wood burning fire. We had taken great pleasure in family and friends visiting us over the holiday season. Now we were ready to resume our quieter lifestyle. As we mused over some of the events of the season, one festive gathering in particular came to mind.

We had arranged a Christmas dinner with friends and family, in a private dining room of a small, charming hotel. We had not seen some of our friends' offspring for several years. It was a delightful time of reminiscence and amaze-ment, observing the level of maturity these young people had achieved. They seemed at ease and comfortable, enjoy-ing life to the fullest, as were their parents and everyone who was there.

As one guest who was new to the group put it, "My gen-eral impression is this lovely group of people is happily at peace with themselves, with others, and with the moment. There seems to be an underlying feeling of contentment and acceptance emanating from everyone; it shows through in their eyes, smiles, voices and body language."

Our granddaughter, who was fourteen at the time, had been invited to the dinner and happily accepted. She was visiting with us for several days during the holiday season, and we were pleased that she wanted to attend. After we introduced her to several adults, she soon found a group of youngsters and was content to chat with them. Occasionally, I glanced over at her to see how she was doing, and observed that she was totally engaged in her conversation with others. She seemed to have no insecurity or unease. I found this rather amazing, based on my own experiences, long ago, as a fourteen year old.

As Ken and I sat before the fire and discussed this event, I remarked that I would not have been as comfortable at a gathering of new people when I was our granddaughter's age. Ken laughingly agreed that he was in the same boat. I related a comment that our granddaughter made to me the next day, after the dinner party.

"I really enjoyed the dinner, Grandma. There was good energy there."

"That's nice, dear. Tell me more."

"Well, I felt safe there, as if I belonged. It was good energy."

And that was the extent of our conversation for the moment. But her words lingered and continued to resonate within me; "good energy."

The next day, she and I went to the local coffee house and the topic came up again. I must admit, I prompted the conversation, as I was intrigued with her comment.

"How do you know its good energy?"

"Well, because it feels good." She looked at me as if to say "duh" but was respectful enough to refrain from actually making the statement.

"So, if you know that was good energy at the dinner party," I carried on, "do you have other experiences when you feel the energy is not so good?"

I knew I was pressing and being nosy, but I was genuinely curious to see what "good energy" meant to her. I would have backed off had she become uncomfortable with the turn of conversation.

She thought for a moment in response to my question, and then said, "Yes. I just had an experience the other day where the energy wasn't so good. The last school day before Christmas holidays, some of my friends skipped school, and went into the city. They asked me to join them, but it didn't feel right, so I didn't go. I wanted to go, but I just didn't feel right about it, so I stayed behind."

She didn't seem concerned about this; she didn't seem to feel that her friends thought any less of her. She just appeared matter of fact about the situation.

Again, this insightful young girl astonished me. She was so casual about "good energy" and "not so good energy". I wondered if she knew the value of recognizing the different tones of energy. Then it dawned on me; she must have realized it at some level, because she didn't accompany her friends. The knowledge was so natural and ordinary; it was no big deal to her.

The situation was such an eye opener. Clearly, the understanding is inherent in her, just as it is inherent in all of us, whether we are educated about this fact or not.

As Ken and I contemplated the wisdom of our granddaughter, we laughingly recalled our own teenage years, when we had behaved in certain ways we knew weren't right. The outcome of our poor conduct was disciplinary action from our parents. Of course, in those days, we had no idea we were the creators of our poor behavior. We would blame our actions on extenuating circumstances. For example; our friends encouraged us to misbehave; we would feel the heat of their disapproval if we didn't go along with the gang. We feared being bullied and treated as outcasts.

When I look back, I know I felt the difference between positive and negative feelings. I know I had an inner voice, often hidden, that I didn't pay attention to. I called that voice, "my conscience." I had no idea that was my wisdom talking; my True Self, cautioning me to take heed.

Now, let's fast forward to another visit from our granddaughter, at 20 years of age. Maturing into a beautiful young woman, still filled with youthful enthusiasm for life; filled with the desire to help at-risk adolescents find their way "home"— to find their True Identity.

How fortunate that so many of our young people are recognizing the power of positive feelings. These youngsters are confident they can be of service to the world, in ways I never considered when I was a young woman. My mind was filled with thoughts of myself, not thoughts of service to others. I wasn't in touch with my inner wisdom, and could not comprehend a world beyond my immediate vision. Innocent of my True Self, I was lost in a narrow reality, filled with angst and concern for my future, which lacked promise and purpose. I know many of my friends felt the same.

Imagine; if more of the world followed their deeper feelings of compassion and purpose, what a harmonious global community we would have. Wouldn't the world be a better place? Isn't this what we are meant to do? Isn't serving others, in whatever capacity unfolds for us in our lives, fulfilling our spiritual pledge to share the gift of wisdom?

Wisdom's Wake-up Call

In life, sometimes it may take a little kick-start for people to continue their development. Inner evolution is never ending; the journey toward more spiritual learning, more understanding, is infinite. Sometimes, we kick-start ourselves, via a realization that we've gotten too comfortable; that we're taking things for granted. There may be times when, in innocence, we begin to believe our own hyperbole and think we know it all; this attitude leads to complacency.

It's important to appreciate that there is more to learn; more perspective to be gained. On occasion, the impetus to change will come from a friend, a colleague, or family member; life has various ways of stimulating inner growth. Often times, we listen; other times, we don't, and the nudge may become a little harder.

When life is going well, it is wonderful to feel grateful, and to enjoy it. We may not even realize when these feelings of gratitude and enjoyment subtly start to shift, and complacency sneaks in. Our appreciation decreases, and, whether we recognize it or not, there is an underlying sense that something is "off."

To put this another way: when we reach a spiritual plateau, we can see for miles, the scenery is great, and we're enjoying the view. We have surely fallen into complacency when we observe that the plateau is flat, and so are our feelings! Just noticing this can give us another chance to grow; we may shake our heads, laugh at how we've fooled ourselves again, and find more gratitude.

On the other hand, we may remain vaguely dissatisfied but unwilling to move, until Divine Mind steps in with a wake-up call (or two or three!), and we begin to realize more spiritual depth. As we awaken, we find ourselves simultaneously moving into another level, a highland beyond the plateau. Our new viewpoint gives us a wider, richer perspective with which to observe and participate in life.

The spiritual nudge, or thump, depending on how drowsy we are, provides a dose of humility, which is just what the doctor ordered. Humility introduces a new sense of quiet, a time of reflection, of listening more than talking. There's an old adage, "God gave you two ears and one mouth so you can listen twice as much as you talk." You learn to listen quietly, with humility, and to talk in silence, communicating and learning with a deep feeling of respect.

The trick, when you get the wake-up call, is not to be embarrassed that you slept in—but to appreciate the call came when it did, so you weren't alarmingly late at all, just a bit lethargic. If you persist in your chagrin, you pay the price of needless struggle. Often times, just a little bit of discomfort is enough to remind you that this is **not** what you want, just as a touch of the flu reminds you to take better care of yourself, and helps you to appreciate your physical health.

As soon as your level of consciousness shifts, you bounce back to deeper feelings, and insightful information comes to you. This knowledge serves as a map, guiding you to the highland. Your mental and spiritual health is restored, and your vision expands.

Please understand, I'm not implying you have to struggle to enrich your understanding of life; not at all. What I'm saying is that the intellect will fight to hold its position, which is where the discomfort comes in. There is a fine balance between experiencing momentary unrest, heeding the message, and moving on—or lingering in distress, and reaping the ensuing feelings. Unhindered by ego restraints, I know you will choose wisely.

Stand Back From the Fire

Many people believe in the myth that you have to struggle in order to grow. While discomfort can be a signal that there is more to learn (as mentioned in the previous chapter, "Wisdom's Wake-up Call"); the sooner we heed the signal, the sooner our discomfort dissipates, and growth occurs.

If you do not heed the signal that initial discomfort sends, you may find yourself mired in a mental struggle. The accompanying stress, in and of itself, is sending an even stronger message: "Enough is enough. It is time to move on." You alone make the decision of whether or not to do that, using the gift of free will.

Let me share an example with you. A multi-national corporation employs Joyce as a senior management consultant. She has enjoyed ten years with this company. Recently, the firm has merged with another organization and there is a shift in power and cultural philosophy. The old firm was a proponent of healthy psychological functioning, and encouraged insight-based learning. The new firm supports programs that seek to promote well-being by way of techniques and modalities.

Joyce struggles to adapt to the new culture without losing her sense of integrity. She feels that if she uses techniques geared toward helping people function in a healthy state of mind, she is being untrue to what she knows. Joyce has a deep understanding that all people have a natural, innate capacity for well-being, and that everyone has the potential to function from a state of mental health and clarity. She knows that techniques actually get in the way of this healthy, insightful process.

The dilemma for Joyce is this: Does she leave, or does she stay with the company? Concern about financial stability naturally plays a big part in her decision, so she stays on while researching and considering other options. The inner struggle continues while she remains with the company. She feels she can't leave, yet she is not happy while she stays. What to do?

Joyce believes that by keeping her "feet in the fire," a term she uses to describe her mental angst, she is motivated to make a change and pursue more fulfilling projects. She feels that because she has some inner knowledge about how the Principles create experience, she should be able to maintain a healthy state of mind during her remaining time with the company. However, the belief that her inner turmoil is somehow productive is sabotaging her mental health, and she is basically unhappy at work.

The question is this: What is she offering her clients, given her state of mind? Granted, when she is doing a team building program, she forgets her troubles and is able to focus on the group she is working with. She feels that she is still able to be helpful. Is the impact as strong?

As time goes on, Joyce begins to feel as if she is between a rock and a hard place. Because her new boss is technique oriented and does not understand the Three Principles approach that Joyce is teaching, he begins to berate her for her lack of modalities. It becomes increasingly difficult for Joyce to continue to share the Principles with her clients. On one hand, she understands that her boss is perplexed by the lack of form of the Principles. On the other hand, he is not interested in learning about them. She could overlook the stress this dilemma created for only so long; something was going to have to give soon.

After a period of time, Joyce could no longer ignore her wisdom. It dawned on her that not only was her impact not as strong in helping her clients, but that the "feet in the fire" mentality was getting her down and keeping her down. Realizing this calmed her, and renewed her commitment to re-connect with her True Self. Once she got in touch with her spiritual core, she knew what to do.

She could see that although she was expressing the same words to introduce the Principles and share information about wisdom, there was not the same feeling of certainty behind them. With humility and honesty, Joyce knew this was because she herself was not living in truth.

Joyce also noticed her personal life was suffering. She was taking the stress from work home to her family. This was the straw that broke the camel's back. She'd had enough. Her family was too important to her; she could not continue working in a company with a culture that was at odds with her own deep commitment of service to others. She was not willing to live in a world of techniques. She had already experienced too much wisdom in her life to deny it any longer.

As if by magic, once Joyce made the decision to leave, an opportunity for a new position was offered to her. A colleague in another organization was promoted to Department Head of Human Resources. He asked Joyce if she would be interested in joining his team, and using the Principles work as a foundation for their training programs. Needless to say, she was thrilled, and eagerly accepted.

When you are functioning from wisdom, you will see the futility of keeping your feet in the fire, as Joyce learned. You will see that it only contributes to your stress. We all go through the fire from time to time, but to stay there doesn't make sense.

If you stand back from the flame, you'll find you're not so hot. When you are cooler, you will be able to think more clearly, and to see more options. Divine Mind doesn't keep us close to the blaze. Our egos do that, insisting we can manage, or we can hold out, until things are just right. Sometimes things don't turn out right until we make a step in the right direction. This is called faith—supported by wisdom. When you listen to your wisdom, the situation unfolds in the most appropriate manner.

The other thing to remember is this: when you are in integrity to what you know is the Truth, wonderful opportunities unfold for you. Prepare yourself for them by allowing your wisdom to emerge. Step forward confidently, with courage and faith. ***See*** that we are living in a world of energy, made into form by our use of thought. Remember, we create our own reality. When we stand back from the fire, we can feel the fresh air of insight, and solutions appear. Let us open up the windows of our mind, and allow the fresh air to rejuvenate us and move us forward.

Exercising Wisdom and Insights

Is it important to examine our thinking, to find out why we feel and behave the way we do? Or is it more significant to know ***that*** we think? And is it even more essential to consider the ***nature*** of Thought? It seems like these are simple questions, each with an easy answer. Let me suggest that the answers may be easy for some, less so for others.

The spiritual nature of the Three Principles is the most vital consideration on our inner journey. As we get glimmers of insight into the true nature of Thought, we come to realize ever more deeply that "we are the thinker." What we think about is less significant than the fact ***that*** we think. Our thinking is what creates our experience in life.

Being aware that "we are the thinker" puts us in the driver's seat, driving where we choose, rather than seated in the passenger's position, going wherever we are driven. As the driver, if we focus our thoughts negatively, we have negative experiences; similarly, if we focus our thoughts in a positive manner, we have positive experiences. The game is in our ball park, and we can hit a home run or we can strike out. It's up to us.

For many, the previous statement will seem elementary; but if you reflect for a moment, you may find a deeper appreciation for the value of this fact. To others, this will be new and edifying data.

What brings new awareness to light is the principle of Consciousness, which helps center our attention on who and what we really are: spiritual beings. As we discover our inner nature, the quality of our thinking is naturally elevated.

Scott, an insurance agent with an intense demeanor, related this story to me during a coaching session. "I am exasperated with my inability to let go of my thinking. My mind is going a million miles a minute. I'm having a difficult time with my boss and with my support staff. I realize I'm probably over analyzing, but the more I examine my thinking to find out what thoughts are triggering my reactions toward them, the more upset I get," he confided. "I know it's my thinking, but at this point I am so tired of trying to figure it out. It's too frustrating!"

"What if I told you that not wanting to "examine" your thinking makes absolute sense, and I applaud you for it?" I said. "Furthermore, what if I told you that not wishing to examine your thoughts is your innate wisdom, telling you this direction is not psychologically healthy?"

Scott pondered this for a few moments, as if he didn't know what to say, and then asked hesitantly, "Are you sure? I took some psychology courses at college, and I thought we were supposed to examine our thinking to see where we went wrong. Are you saying not to do that?"

"Yes, I am. It's not about examining your thoughts and trying to figure out which thought is triggering which reaction. That is intellectual exploration of the content of thought. The danger in this is that people get caught up in their thinking and spiral downward with feelings of guilt, blame, judgment and so on.

"Consider the nature of Thought, and that Thought creates our moment to moment reality. As we begin to look at the essence of Thought, we will find our way home, inside our own psyche, where our innate mental health resides. This automatically brings about healthier thinking. We don't have to do anything, other than allow healthier thoughts to emerge. Well-being is our default setting.

"However, if you persist in analyzing your thoughts, you are playing in hazardous territory; you are riding in rough water where there are no answers, only more questions."

"That is an interesting theory, but it seems too simple," Scott protested, shaking his head and looking confused. "I remember our instructor telling us at college that to understand our behavior we must know what thought triggers that behavior."

"How does that process make you feel, Scott?"

"It makes me feel like I've done something wrong."

"Well, here's a gift for you. You've got all the right answers already, inside of you. All I'm asking you to do is relax and reflect on the nature of Thought, which is formless energy that we, as thinking creatures, have the ability to turn into form, into behavior. How does that sound to you?"

Again there was silence, this time rich with feeling. "Well," Scott said thoughtfully, "I've never thought about this before, but it seems exciting and confusing, all at the same time. Relaxing and reflection does seem a lot easier and less painful than analysis. It feels hopeful. But does it really work? It's been my experience that to gain anything worthwhile, you must work at it."

"Tell me, Scott, have you ever had an insight; an 'aha' moment, when things came clear to you, and you knew what to do to resolve a troubling situation? Has a creative idea occurred to you that you had never thought of before?"

"Yes, to both your questions. I seem to do my best thinking when I'm trout fishing on the lake, or tying flies for my fishing hobby. I often get ideas that seem to come out of the blue. Those ideas are helpful to me at work, and they always seem to succeed. But what has that got to do with examining or not examining my thinking?"

"My point is, the insights you have when you are relaxed, tying flies or fishing, are coming from your innate wisdom; from Divine Mind. You didn't work at it; there was no effort to get those insights. Would you agree?"

"You know, Elsie, I've never considered this before, but it is true. Those flashes of clarity just happened naturally, spontaneously. It never occurred to me they came from what you call innate wisdom. I've never heard of innate wisdom. My definition of wisdom would be based on learning from the experiences you get in life. Yet, there seems to be something to what you're saying, because I've certainly had those intuitive moments."

Clearly, Scott was intrigued so I expanded upon his comments. "That deep, insightful process unfolds when we stop looking at our thinking with a jaundiced, examining eye. Instead, consider the nature of Thought. I know that sometimes it sounds ephemeral to consider the nature of the Principles, but it is extremely valuable. We are touching the very essence of life when we do this. It frees our personal mind from all the clutter of self-analytical thought, thus opening the door to insight."

I looked at Scott closely to see if he was still following my train of thought. His brow was furrowed but his eyes were glued on mine.

I carried on, "Insight provides us with answers. It is a gentle way to move forward. If we experience struggle, it is of our own making, by persisting in trying to figure things out. Trust your wisdom to do the job effortlessly and with far more efficiency."

"I'll have to consider that," Scott said. "It certainly sounds easier, and I do value the insights I've had when fishing. I'm just not sure I can have insights at work. I'm not as relaxed and I'm too busy. It seems to me that my mind is too wrapped up in the details of work for insights to happen. How do I get past that?"

"Did it take a long time for your insights to occur to you, while fishing?"

"No; as I said, they just popped into my head."

"That's right. Insights aren't about time. They happen in a flash of clarity. Insight is always available; at work, on the freeway driving to work, in the middle of the lake. Insight unfolds in an instant. The more we acknowledge and recognize that we have this inherent ability, the more we are gifted to use it. It's like exercising a muscle; it becomes stronger, more useful, more flexible, and able to be used anywhere, not just in the gym."

"Well, I'll exercise my insights and let you know how it goes," Scott said cheerfully.

A month later, Scott called and asked if he could drop by my office to talk. He sounded eager, and we arranged a time for our next session.

Scott bounded through the door with a boyish grin on his face. I was struck by how much younger he looked, the lines of stress and heaviness replaced by a smile. He seemed light-hearted and at ease.

"Thanks so much for seeing me. It's been amazing this last month. I don't know what's happening, but the office is running like a charm. The people around me seem comfortable, and more productive in their work. My relationship with my boss is getting better; although we've still got a ways to go. Things are really good."

"Why do you think that is?"

"I don't know why."

"Take a guess."

"I'm getting out of people's way, letting them do their jobs, not micro-managing like I used to."

"That's great. But where are those results coming from?"

"I'm slowing down, more at peace within myself."

"Where is that coming from?"

"I don't know."

"Could it be you are finding more understanding and wisdom?"

"Well, yes, I guess so. I am having more insightful thinking, where things just occur to me in the moment, even at work. I don't have to go fishing to have insights," Scott chuckled. "But I'm not sure how long it's going to last."

I burst out laughing at how quickly Scott's face changed, as he wondered if his new found wisdom was going to disappear. "Not to worry, Scott. Your wisdom is infinite, as is everyone's. I'll pass on a tip that will help you to nurture and sustain your inner resources, if you'd like to hear it."

Scott nodded his head, "Please carry on," he said with fervor.

"It's important to acknowledge your wisdom in action, my friend. The change in the way you are behaving is evidence that your understanding of the Principles is working for you. Acknowledgement leads to more wisdom unfolding. We're back to the exercise analogy. The more you use wisdom and insights, the healthier, more consistent and sustainable your state of mind will be. You are living in well-being more of the time. Well-being becomes a part of life because it already ***is*** part of you. Often, we just aren't aware of our inner resources and, consequently, don't use them appropriately. As I said in our previous session, well-being is our default setting.

We sat quietly for a few moments, each absorbed in our own thoughts. As Scott got up to leave, he shook my hand; then gave me a hug. "I'm forever in your debt," he said. I was moved by his comment, but pointed him back to his own wisdom. "You've changed because of your own insights, Scott. I'm delighted to have witnessed the transformation in you."

Different Levels of Consciousness

It's natural that people feel concerned when their well-being takes a dip south. They may fear that the good feeling will not return. They may blame themselves, or others, for not being able to maintain a healthy state of mind; or perhaps they fall into the trap of blaming circumstances.

Identifying external factors as a cause for low moods seems like a logical assumption; as human beings, we are accustomed to reasoning our way out of difficulty. Understanding that we use the Principles to create our personal reality helps us see that we all experience different levels of consciousness at different times: higher, lower, and an infinite range in between. The ebb and flow of the quality of our thinking is linked to our level of consciousness. Realizing that we are the creator of our experience provides us with the spiritual power to minimize our low periods. We become the observer of our state of mind, rather than a victim of our negative feelings.

Another way of viewing this is to see that our stressful feelings, such as anxiety, worry, doubt, jealousy, resentment, and so forth, are all coming from insecure thoughts. Instead of being concerned and analytical about each separate thought and feeling, you can simply see insecure thoughts as the base cause of insecure feelings. When you go back inside and re-engage your True Identity, your mind is freed of distracting thoughts. The moment understanding takes the place of insecurity, the unhealthy feelings are eliminated, gently and without struggle.

Viewing low moods can be like watching the tide go out. When you see the tide roll out, you don't blame it or judge it for being low. You simply acknowledge it as a natural gravitational process. Interestingly enough, when the tide is out, you can walk along the beach much further, observing new shells and rock formations never before noticed. You can also see garbage in places and clean it up. In like manner, when the psychological mood is low, you can take the opportunity to survey what needs tidying up in the human landscape.

You may say that when you are feeling in a low mood you are not open to exploring new vistas. That may be so, but consider the idea; when the mind is open to possibility, new thinking and new understanding occurs. Doesn't it sound worth a try? It's much better than dwelling on the low mood and lingering longer than necessary.

Another analogy comes to mind regarding low moods. Observe your low mood in the same way you monitor the red light coming on in your vehicle, indicating that the oil is low and needs refilling. You don't blame or judge the oil, or the red light. You refill the oil container, and the red light disappears. Understand that your low mood is an indicator that you need to nourish your soul, refilling with calmness, and the low mood will vanish. Even considering the idea will give your mind some respite from insecure thinking.

Jean was struggling with her low moods. She felt like a failure whenever her mood level dropped. She had taken classes in the Three Principles understanding, and thought that the training would prevent her from having low moods. Jean told me she was disappointed when her mood level fell from the high peak she had been experiencing. She believed that once she understood the Principles, her state of mind would be consistently healthy, and she would never feel low again. With this kind of thinking and expectations, her mood slumped even lower. Jean was making herself miserable with all her judgmental thoughts.

Jean was dismissive about the helpfulness of seeing how your low moods act as a psychological red light, indicating it is time for a "calm and chill" refill. "I should know better," Jean stated emphatically. "I've been learning the Principles for two years; I know I can do better. I try to think positive and sometimes it works, but not always.

"My life has completely transformed, except for these low mental states that keep creeping back into my mind. It's insidious, like dandelion weeds that turn to seed, and are caught by the wind and blown around the yard. I feel as if my mind is cluttered with weeds, and I'm buffeted by the wind. I thought the Principles were supposed to strengthen us, not make us weaker," she said in an accusatory tone. "I feel like I've lost control over my thoughts."

Jean was caught in a web of her own making. She was a high achiever who had accomplished much in life with dedication, commitment and will power. It appeared she had learned about the Three Principles on an intellectual level, and was trying to practice them as a technique. She was "willing" her low moods to disappear, and it wasn't working. What she didn't realize was that if she relaxed and calmed down, her level of consciousness would naturally rise, understanding would emerge, and she would be able to see her moods with neutrality.

Trying to think positive thoughts when you are feeling low is an impossible task. When you "try" to think positive, you are denying your innate mental health, and the trying actually gets in the way of releasing your resilience. "Trying" means you have to constantly remind yourself to be optimistic, and it can wear you out. Trying to think positive puts a strain on you by filling your mind with personal thoughts. Insightful thoughts, full of inner wisdom, can't get through the blockage of a thought logjam. "Trying" gets in the way of "being."

The best thing you can do is to do nothing; trust that your consciousness is ready to help you, and just observe that you are in a different mood. This neutral observation is the role of the Principle of Consciousness. When we are able to observe with neutrality, it means we've had a shift into a higher level of consciousness. It is amazing how this shift will calm you down.

When you see different levels of consciousness as a natural process in our spiritual and psychological make-up, the naturalness takes away the downhearted feeling of low moods. This knowledge adds another dimension of sustainability to your well-being.

In fact, the secret to help shift you into a higher state of mind is to be grateful to see the red light. If you didn't heed the red light in your vehicle telling you the oil needs refilling, you might burn up the car's engine. In like manner, if you don't heed the red light of your psychological low tide, you may burn out your engine!

To carry on with my story about Jean, about a month went by before she called to share how she was getting along. "At first when you were telling me about the role of Consciousness, I was resistant and dubious. Although I was taken with the analogy of low tides, I wondered if this was a form of denial. An insight began to take shape in my mind and shifted my perspective. I saw that my thinking was attached to fear and insecurity. The insight allowed me to accept my low moods as an ordinary process of life, and they became less significant to me. My state of mind no longer consumed me.

"I can't get over it. It seems paradoxical; the moment I understood my low moods were attached to anxiety, the mental anguish simply evaporated," she said, sounding slightly bewildered. "The moment of giving up, and finding out that low moods are simply different moods, put me in the frame of mind of becoming a student of life, rather than a victim of low tides.

"I had thought that acceptance was a cop-out, so I couldn't agree that my low moods were as natural as the ocean's low tides. I felt I needed to fight them to survive," Jean said passionately, "and that acceptance was a sign of weakness. Now

I see acceptance as a gift, and an opportunity to grow. It's a matter of being patient and letting go of your own preconceived notion of what low moods are." Her voice softened, "The change in my outlook has filled me with feelings of gratitude, and marked an irrevocable turning point in my life."

Jean's story illustrates the shift from an intellectual understanding of the Principles to realizing a spiritual fact. We are gifted with the mystical power to create our experience moment to moment. When we are consumed by negative thoughts, low moods are what we experience. When we live with gratitude—as Jean put it, "being a student of life"—we find the universe consistently provides us with continuing education assignments—to learn and to grow, to become a wiser human, just "being".

Life's Assignments

Isn't it interesting to see how life provides us with opportunities to learn and grow? In a manner of speaking, it's as if Divine Mind is giving us homework to see how well we "walk our talk." Viewing challenging times from this perspective helps neutralize the situation, and gives us a sense of objectivity from which to discover the best solution.

Life's assignments may not all be challenging, but I would suggest that every day there is something new to learn; perhaps a softer, gentler way of observing life, that broadens your perspective and provides more clarity. The assignment may take the shape of a discussion between co-workers, who are not in complete accord. A difference of opinion can offer a wonderful opportunity to see how to come into alignment; or, if that is not possible, to agree that it is okay to respectfully disagree.

Life's assignments present us with floor space to walk our talk in a way that brings to life insights we've had, resulting in helpful change. The positive energy of insight not only enhances our own knowledge, but also affects other people, helping them discover more of their own wisdom.

Let me illustrate what I mean. In a Three Principles training I conducted with a group who work with incarcerated youth, there were a couple of phrases that the staff used that were new to me. One expression was "solid object," meaning that in a difficult situation, the detention officers are taught to remain calm and focused. The idea is to maintain a solid bearing, a calm presence, and not to get angry when the youth get angry, act out or get violent. The purpose of this solid bearing was to defuse the situation. The idea sounded good, but often times the employees got caught up in the confrontational event, and difficulties arose.

I asked the officers to educate me on what the "solid object process" looked like, and I must admit that I wondered at some of the things they said. I was dubious about the way they were trained to handle these tense situations. Apparently, they were taught to escalate along with the youth and to meet the kids where they were mentally, but at the same time maintain their calm presence. I really didn't see how it was possible for them to escalate their state of mind yet remain calm. The idea seemed totally at cross purposes.

However, for some reason, the words "solid object" continued to resonate with me. It flashed across my mind that the ability to live in calm is an outcome of innate mental health, which is part of the Three Principles understanding. The significant difference is that we recognize mental health and wisdom as innate; something we are born with, not taught.

Despite being poles apart, the group and I were able to bridge the gap between the different terms—solid object, innate mental health and wisdom—in a way that allowed all of us to learn and grow. We all had different ways of expressing our understanding. Ultimately, the group saw that "solid object," when grounded in innate wisdom, was a completely different process, which elicited a far more positive response from the youth.

The trainees took a deeper look at what the Principles brought to the table. They began to see that the Principles lead us to wisdom, and that wisdom is a spiritual gift that can be counted on, all the time. Wisdom offers mental stability during crisis because it is inherent and all-knowing.

Another slogan from this group that caught my ear was "handle with care." This expression relates to the manner of handling young residents in detention who may need to be physically restrained during a violent episode, as protection from injuring themselves or others.

As we explored how this procedure was done, what struck me was how important it would be for a staff member to have a sustained, healthy state of mind when having to restrain someone. If that course of action was necessary, whoever was restricting a detainee would need to be able to remain calm. Obviously, an officer who was feeling stressed would not be thinking as clearly, and perhaps be a little more reactive than necessary.

In other words, if an employee was having a bad day, even if they were trying their best to remain calm and collected, it's likely the treatment of the youngster might not be as sensitive as when the worker was in a healthy state of mind. I know from my own experiences as a parent that when I was feeling stressed, I took the kids' behavior personally. At times, I found it difficult to remain calm and composed. Once I learned how the human experience is created, my ability to handle stressful situations improved considerably. I no longer regarded the kids as being out to get me, but listened more to the non-verbal message of individuals crying out for attention, crying out to be "seen."

It stands to reason that without an understanding of how our thinking creates our experience, the ability to sustain a healthy state of mind is hit and miss. The lack of knowledge creates a good deal of stress. When employees experience chronic stress, staff burnout occurs, and patience is rare. The kids tend to experience more discipline and time-out issues, and a higher rate of recidivism occurs.

The counselors and staff I met with were very conscientious and cared deeply about the kids they had in their care. With their new found knowledge of the Three Principles, they went back to their jobs with more optimism, viewing their youthful charges with fresh understanding and compassion.

The officers saw that even the worst offenders had the capacity for mental health. The adults' shift in perspective brought forth a new way of interfacing with the young detainees, which encouraged them to respond in a more positive manner.

Instead of focusing, as usual, on the juvenile's poor behavior, the officers began to see beyond behavior. They saw deep inside the youngsters, where their true spiritual core resides, and drew upon their innate mental health. This new perspective of the officers prompted the youth to view their own potential in a way they hadn't before. It helped them to see that they were fundamentally sound.

It was a drastic reversal for these incarcerated kids, to go from seeing themselves as broken and needing to be fixed, to seeing themselves as basically mentally healthy. As the teens learned about the Principles, supported by staff, and began to feel more positive and hopeful, their behavior changed for the better. They began to see they had more options to move forward in their lives, to become happy, healthy, productive teenagers. They began to help each other as peer-counselors. I witnessed several incidents where a classmate was able to get through and help a particularly uncommunicative child, whom a counselor had not been able to reach.

There was another major change in the employees' attitudes, beyond the way they treated the kids; the way they treated each other changed. Not only were they able to access their "solid object" state of mind more of the time, but the other phrase, "handle with care," became imbued with new meaning. There was more sensitivity toward one another, as well as toward the youth. Deeper listening, less judgment, more light-heartedness and laughter, evoked more harmony and cooperation amongst the whole group, adults and youth.

The organizational culture was beginning to change from the inside-out. Rather than using techniques, they began to utilize inner wisdom. The organization actually implemented on-going Three Principles training, continuing to offer it to all departments, as well as making it part of the orientation for new employees. The success of the training in relieving stress, burnout, and promoting well-being to employees and detainees, elicited interest from outside organizations and clinics, who requested training for their personnel.

I went back to my life with more respect for the workers in the trenches. Grateful to have been allowed into their world, I was honored to introduce the Three Principles as a foundation for enhancing their work. Their genuine commitment to serving the youth in need is commendable.

I also saw, with fresh eyes, how important it is to listen with open ears to find a place of alignment, rather than disagreement. Alignment enriches the relationship between trainer and trainees and enhances the educational process. I leaned from them and they learned from me. The learning was mutually beneficial and very rewarding. It was a life assignment for me that I will always cherish and never forget.

Here's another example of life's assignments. Although in a totally different industry, the context is similar; an individual hurting and needing to be "seen." Jeff, a friend of mine, related this story at lunch the other day. "I'm consulting as a construction manager," he told me, "with one of the owners of a large shopping center that is undergoing substantial renovations. I've been struggling with maintaining my healthy state of mind. The owner is caught up with the details of the project, including the fact that it is already way over budget, even before they've started the major renovations. That is why they hired me; to work through some of the mess and see if we can't get back on track.

"The owner has gotten angry several times; not at me, but he takes it out on me. He's angry about the increase in budget and many others issues. At first I didn't get hooked when he shouted at me. I understood that he was just venting, and didn't take it personally. Nevertheless, it was getting increasingly harder to maintain my calmness.

"Then I remembered you and I talking about "life's assignments" and I realized that this situation was exactly that: life's assignment to walk my talk more. What an opportunity!" Jeff said, rolling his eyes dramatically. "Seeing these circumstances as an assignment provided by life gave me food for thought. The shift in my perspective immediately lifted me out of my personal thinking so I could see the owner as a level of consciousness, rather than just seeing him as the angry owner. The spiritual shift in my understanding neutralized and calmed my feelings toward him. I felt compassion for the struggle he was going through."

"How did your client respond to your calming down?" I asked.

"It's weird," Jeff responded. "The man seemed startled that I didn't react to his anger, and then he calmed down. We were able to get a lot of work done. One of the many things I continue to learn and appreciate from understanding the Three Principles is that approaching my clients with unconditional regard and service is what makes the most sense to me now."

Jeff's story about how his insight changed the way he approached his client really speaks to the value of being a "solid object" and "handling with care." What will our next assignment be? What will we learn from life's assignment? Who knew that homework could be such fun!

The Power of Noticing

The power of noticing comes from the principle of Consciousness. It seems a simple thing, the ability to notice, but often the ability is undervalued or misunderstood. Notice what, you might ask? Become aware of how the human experience is created through the spiritual Principles of Mind, Consciousness and Thought. Notice the feeling attached to the experience.

For example, Nathan had an interaction with Ben, a colleague, which was tense and stressful. Nathan defended his position and refused to listen to Ben's point of view. He felt he was in the right, and that Ben wasn't seeing clearly. When Ben tried to explain his position, Nathan walked out of the room. He justified his attitude by saying, "Ben just doesn't get it, and I don't have time to waste on this nonsense."

Later, when Nathan calmed down, he realized he could have handled things differently. He recognized that the feeling in the interaction had been "off." Instead of being grateful for noticing this, he began to berate himself for not paying attention to the tone of the conversation earlier, while it was happening. Had he been more aware of what was going on, he thought regretfully, the event might have rolled out differently. He felt upset that he had missed an opportunity to communicate more effectively with Ben.

As Nathan calmed down once again, and his level of consciousness shifted, he began to understand that his ego had been challenged. With rueful humor, he realized his earlier lack of gratitude; immediately, a deep feeling of appreciation arose within him. Nathan had his first glimmer that the feeling of gratefulness is released with insight.

It is up to us not to diminish that feeling by judging ourselves harshly for not doing better.

An important point to consider is this: the significance of "noticing" means that Consciousness is alive and functioning, despite our ego or personal thinking. Think about it—we can relax and trust our own wisdom more all the time. Even when our personal thinking gets in the way, there is another level of awareness, a spiritual awareness, which is going on behind the scenes. Consciousness is a wonderful, mystical gift that we want to cherish. Rather than reproaching ourselves because we didn't notice the feeling quickly enough, we can move right to gratefulness that we saw it at all!

I recall a time when I was working in a community in south-central Los Angeles. The residents, who were part of a Principle-based leadership development program, had asked me to host a community meeting. The purpose was to explore how to advance ideas for developing home and community-based businesses in the area.

In attendance were many residents, community and business leaders, and potential funders. Also present was a business consultant who was knowledgeable about the Three Principles, as his own organization was involved in culture change via the Principles. I remember being on edge because of the importance of the gathering, and recall that I had expectations regarding the outcome.

As the meeting progressed, a debate arose over which community group would operate the bus for transporting residents to various events. At first I remained impartial, and just observed what was going on, aware that the tone of the meeting was dropping rapidly. Then I became engaged in the debate and soon forgot about the tone. Before long, I was arguing in earnest about which group should handle the transportation. I had lost my objectivity and become quite subjective. Not listening to others' opinions but only holding to my own, of course I was unable to bring the meeting to consensus.

Fortunately, the business consultant sitting across the conference table caught my eye, and gently intervened. He suggested we take a break and come back to the discussion after refreshments. In that moment, I realized what had happened and how unhealthy the feeling of interaction had become. I felt rather sheepish, but the business consultant graciously made light of my chagrin. After the break, I was able to function from a healthier level, and we ended up having a very creative discussion. A mutually agreeable solution developed as to which group would operate the business of transportation.

Upon reflection, the meeting was very helpful to me. Once I had moved past my ego and self-interest, I could see how damaging not noticing the tone of communication could be. While I was engaged in the argument of who was right, who was wrong, and who should do what, I was invested solely in my own agenda—working for myself rather than for the good of the community.

The event was an eye opener, for me and for the community. They had noticed that I had become invested in the outcome. They also were aware when I had a shift in my level of consciousness, and was able to carry on hosting the meeting from a healthy state of mind. That incident revealed more about the power of the Principles than all the teaching I had done prior to that gathering.

Another example comes to mind, when I was working in the same community, planning a retreat for a core group of residents who were participating in the leadership program. The idea was to invite community police and other key players in the area, to strategize a plan with the residents for crime prevention. We were delighted that two local gang members also agreed to participate.

We had a connection with a hotel in a nearby city, and they offered us, free of charge, accommodations, meals, and a conference room. We were thrilled with the generous gift, and everything was moving along smoothly. Then word got out to the rest of the community that a select group of residents were getting to go to this fancy resort, with free food and rooms. Soon the demand from other residents to go along became unreasonable. We could not accommodate everyone who wanted to go. The feeling became uncomfortable and awkward, but we did the best we could to alleviate the unrest that was developing.

Finally, things seemed to settle down, and the invited participants met at the hotel to begin the retreat. To my dismay, several uninvited people showed up. They were part of a group of residents who tended to be negative and contentious, and not in favor of the leadership program. They had been watching from the sidelines as community residents who had learned about the Principles were changing, becoming more confident and successful.

I was unsure how to begin the retreat. Several of the invited residents started to grumble about the uninvited guests. My uncertainty about what to do increased. One resident whispered in my ear that I should ask them to leave, and my discomfort grew. I was beginning to think this was a retreat from hell!

After a good deal of procrastination, I took the initiative and informed our new guests, privately, that this retreat was only for the residents in the leadership program. We simply didn't have the accommodations to house more people. I told them that perhaps another time we would be able to open the retreat to more members of the community. They looked at me with disdain, disagreed with my explanation, and said that because they were part of the community, they had every right to be there. The tension escalated. All eyes were on me.

Then, in a moment of clarity, the thought raced across my mind that something was wrong with this picture. Here we were, looking for leadership in the community, and these few people had taken it upon themselves to join us. That certainly was leadership! All I had focused on was that they weren't part of the plan, rather than considering what they could bring to the table. It didn't matter that others thought they were there simply because of the free rooms and food. Candidly, I had felt the same but now I realized that it was more important to give the uninvited residents a chance, and involve them in the program.

I invited our guests to join us and we all sat in chairs placed in a big circle. We sat quietly for a few minutes until peace enfolded us. I shared my gratitude that we had such a diverse group turn out for our event. Coming together, with a feeling of wanting the best for the whole community, not just a part of the community, was our goal. Gradually, people began to share their thoughts and feelings about wanting to live and work together in harmony, wanting to see each other with new eyes, to be more forgiving.

A gang member spoke up, commenting that he would never have believed he could have sat in the same room with a police officer, whom he had always considered his enemy. "Now," he said, "I feel like we're on the same team. I don't know for how long, but for now, it's cool!" People chuckled at his comment, and the sharing became more open and light-hearted.

The retreat from hell turned out to be a retreat in heaven. Ideas and insights generated in that harmonious setting propelled the community to sponsor an event called, "Hands Around our Community", a crime prevention strategy that was written up in the Los Angeles Times, August 10, 1997.

"A Neighborhood Reclaimed" is the title of the article, which is subtitled: "Cleanup, community policing and crime drop help ease fear of residents near Avalon Gardens. Problems still exist, but people are getting to know one another."

The reporter credits Three Principles based education with "train[ing] tenants to be self-sufficient, build self-esteem and take on leadership roles in their community."

He quotes one resident saying, "'There's more hope.'"

What a blessing to be aware when the feeling is off, to be aware of what we are contributing to the situation. The feeling is of primary importance. And in the feeling, there is immediate information that helps you to be in service, in a way that ego would not allow. You go beyond ego to true service, rather than self-service.

The candor we gain through insight leads to gratitude. The more we are grateful for the gift of Consciousness, the more our consciousness is accessed, paving the way for learning, in all its disguises. Events that look as if they lack opportunity suddenly appear rich with learning. Such is the power of noticing.

Take the High Road

There are times in everyone's life when the past rears its head and looks us in the face, taunting us with old, insecure thoughts and emotions. Without understanding the nature of emotions and where they come from, insecure thoughts can be very compelling. Our usage of the Three Principles produces a reality that is convincingly real.

Understanding how we create our experience, in the moment, provides us with a safeguard. This knowledge prevents us from taking negative thoughts, even ones that seem very real at the time, too seriously for very long. It gives us perspective, allowing us to see that we don't have to "work" unconstructive thoughts into an emotional pit of quicksand. It is far better to take the high road, bypassing the booby trap of unhelpful thinking.

It comes down to choice: continuing to dwell on pessimistic thoughts, and making them real, or choosing to move forward and have fresh thinking in the moment. I'm not saying it's always easy. When we are gripped by our thinking, the hold our thoughts have on us is tenacious. It can seem as if we are engulfed in a quagmire, struggling for freedom. An understanding of the Three Principles is like a board lying across the bog, which we can grasp and use to pull ourselves out. Then we can take the high road.

A case in point: A committee of three is given the task of planning an event, to raise funds for the charity sponsored by their organization. The three members had arranged last year's occasion; the planning had been far from harmonious. The group wonders why they have been selected to once again stage the charity affair. They dread working together, and are looking for a way to avoid it. When they query their boss, they are told in no uncertain terms that they are required to do this as part of their civic duty. Perhaps this will be an opportunity for them to learn something new.

Jason says, "It seems to me we're stuck with this job, so we may as well get on with it. The sooner we get working on this, the sooner it's over."

Eva responds, "I agree. My desk is loaded with work, and this is not my favorite thing to be doing right now."

Susan mutters to herself while the other two are talking.

They all glance at each other for a moment, then look away. They toss out ideas based on what they had done last year. No one listens. An uneasy feeling pervades their meeting. They wade forward with more ideas repeated from the previous year. They are getting nowhere fast.

Finally, they come up with some ideas that they can live with, and adjourn the meeting until the next day. Their conversation the following day turns to last years' event. Grappling with the details, Jason reminds Susan of a situation she had neglected to follow through on. The tone of the meeting quickly deteriorates. Susan retaliates by pointing out that if Jason had helped her as he was supposed to, the circumstances wouldn't have occurred. Soon, Jason and Susan are arguing with some ferocity. Definitely, they are not taking the high road...

Eva looks on as this heated discussion is taking place and then calmly says, "You know, it isn't doing us any good to be bringing up the past. Let's just move on, and see what makes sense now." Eva's two co-workers, after a bit more grumbling, agree; the group settles down to once again look at various strategies, and the meeting progresses more smoothly. They all agree to take on certain tasks, meet in a few days, and brief each other.

Their next meeting starts off on a positive note. The team has accomplished much of what they needed to do and are pleased with one another's reports. Susan comments on how much easier this meeting is going than the last one. Jason quips, "Well, that is because you've done your job this time, not like last year when you didn't follow through."

There is an abrupt silence, and then Susan swings back with, "Yes, well this time, I had help with my project. The staff was there for me, not like you, promising and not delivering."

Jason is just about to counter when Eva interrupts and says gently, "Here we go again, back into the past. What's happening here? What are we doing?"

There is a pause, and then Susan says bluntly, "We're working it!" A moment of silence occurs; then everyone bursts out laughing, and the tension dissipates.

When laughter has mellowed out the group, Eva mentions she has been reading a new book on leadership based on Three Principles. "The author talked a great deal about the tone of meetings, and how important it is to have a positive atmosphere. The book states that we use the Three Principles to create our feelings. It really makes sense to me.

"I want to create a positive environment in my life. Seeing the reactive behavior that occurs in our meetings when the tone is off has been an eye opener to me. I don't want to live in negativity; in the office or in my home life. I never noticed the tone so much before reading that book. I much prefer the positive direction in which our discussion was going, before the last few minutes. When the feeling is positive, we listen to each other more. We're more creative and accomplish more, and we have fun doing it. That's how I want our meetings to be."

"You have a point, Eva. I was enjoying our conversation and feeling that we were achieving many of our objectives, until Jason said what he did to me," responds Susan.

"Now just a minute, don't go blaming me for the way the meetings—"

"Hold it right there," interjects Eva. "We're doing it again! We're going back into the past and blaming each other. Let's just stop it and keep to the moment. Didn't you both enjoy the earlier discussion?" Both heads nod. "Then I'm for moving forward and discussing, in a healthy manner, what needs to be done." The feeling is somewhat subdued, but respectful; soon they adjourn, after agreeing to another date to finalize the plans.

As time went on, Eva shared the materials of Sydney Banks, as well as the leadership book based on the Three Principles. As the group learned about their true nature, and gained spiritual power, the meetings continued to improve. More often than not, laughter could be heard coming from the room. Employees walking down the hallway would pop their heads in and inquire, "What's so funny?" There were occasions when one or another of the committee dipped their paddle into the past, but they were learning they were more productive when their state of mind was healthy. Respect and trust were in place, paving the way for harmony and cooperation.

Equally important, the team was realizing they didn't like the feeling when they waded into the murky water of unhealthy thinking. Their tolerance for negativity had lessened considerably, so they didn't linger long. They were well on their way to the high road of success without stress.

Our Inner Coach

It is so important to understand that mental health exists within all people, from the day we are born. You have heard the term "innate mental health" in relation to the Three Principles. This term is synonymous with wisdom, True Self, common sense, inner resiliency, inner strength, inner resources, well-being... and the list goes on. Innate mental health is a powerful spiritual gift. Not everyone gives credence to this, or comprehends the enormous value of having a built-in "coach."

As people get in touch with their spiritual core, their world opens up to more beauty. They experience more understanding of themselves and others. Increased peace of mind, creativity, productivity, and a general sense of well-being are released. The phrase *joie de vivre* comes to life.

The evidence of innate mental health is this: When you point people to their True Identity, and they start to access their wisdom, their lives change for the better. They see life from a different perspective, and everything is transformed. A whole new world is created from the inside-out, via the Three Principles we are blessed with. How could this happen, if we didn't have mental health already within us?

As written in the previous chapter, "Take the High Road", we always have a choice in whether we will access our wisdom. We always have a choice in how we use the Principles. What we are discovering is, the more consistently we use our spiritual resources, the more readily available they are. Why would we continue to live in unhealthy feelings when we can live in well-being? Mental health is our birthright!

The following story illustrates this point. Sharon, a new client, suffers from panic attacks. She calls me for some phone coaching. After the preliminaries are out of the way, Sharon tells me her previous counselor has told her to "feel the feeling of panic, and it will pass." The counselor tells her that panic is a thought, and the thoughts she has been having will pass, if she doesn't hang on to them. The latter advice sounds clear enough; however, the client has heard only the first part of the direction: "Feel the panic." Sharon tells me the advice doesn't feel good. She feels stressed because she can't let go of her fearful thoughts.

When I listen to Sharon's plight, I hear her wisdom coming through as she tells me she doesn't want to feel panic. She is absolutely right, and more power to her! To encourage the feeling of panic, no matter that the advice is coupled with describing the role of thought, escalates unhealthy thinking—the very thing we want to move away from.

When I direct Sharon to her mental health, pointing to her own recognition that "feeling her panic" didn't feel good, she can hardly hear me. Her mind is filled with unhelpful thoughts, and there is no space left to "hear." I continue to share the value of discovering the true nature of who we really are at our core; suddenly she hears something and her spirits rise. When I inquire what she caught, she cannot express herself.

We carry on with our session, and Sharon relates another example of her life. She shares a story of being on the freeway, and having a panic attack. In the midst of her fright she is able to monitor herself. At the first exit she pulls off, stops the car, and waits until she calms down. Then she carries on with her trip, shaken, but capable of continuing.

In telling me this, Sharon is initially focused on her terror. What I hear is her wisdom. I am impressed by her ability to do damage control, having the inner power to pull off at the nearest exit, without harming herself or others.

I tell her this but she is hard pressed to pay attention. I stay quiet for a few minutes. Gradually, her consciousness shifts, her mood elevates, and she hears her inner coach. "What just happened?" Sharon asks.

We continue our phone discussion by exploring the principle of Consciousness. I point out how Consciousness is always working behind the scenes, and is there to help us; particularly, it seems, in times of need. I explain as best I can how we use the spiritual Principles of Mind, Consciousness and Thought, working in unison, to create our feelings; a spectrum of feelings, from fear to calm, and everything in between. We have free will to choose what thoughts we entertain, although sometimes it feels as if have no choice; the thoughts are spinning through our mind so rapidly. We discuss how, despite her panic, her inner coach was at work, guiding her to safety. We agree about how remarkable it is that you can always count on wisdom. What a relief to know we have an inner safeguard, protecting us.

Sharon relates another example about being asked to sing a song at a party. Her background as a professional vocalist has fallen by the wayside because of her panic attacks. She initially declines the invitation to perform; however, she is pressed to accept, and reluctantly agrees. During her song, accompanied by a pianist, Sharon forgets a phrase. She hums along with the music until the words come to her, and then she carries on.

Sharon describes to me her fearful thoughts of panic. "Tell me how your wisdom shows up in your story," I counter.

Sharon pauses, considers for a moment, and then exclaims, "When I forgot the words, hummed along with the music, and finished my song! Personally, I was terrified, but somehow I managed to carry on."

"Yes, that's right!" I proclaimed.

"Wow. That is quite amazing! I had no idea our inner health worked like that. I've heard some performers talk about their anxiety before going on stage. Yet, somehow they come through their pre-show jitters, and perform beautifully. Who knew everyone has a built-in coach on stand-by, called innate mental health? Talk about a performance you can count on!"

We chuckled at the image of each of us having an inner stand-by coach. "What else in your story stands out as evidence of your inner confidence, coming from connecting with your True Self?" I inquire.

"I don't know. Give me a minute. I've never really thought about these kinds of things before."

After a lengthy pause, Sharon says in a thoughtful tone, "I guess it's the fact I even agreed to perform. I was anxious about it, and yet I still sang. When I think about it, it's really remarkable! It does speak to an inner strength and resiliency I didn't know I had." With a huge sigh, Sharon says, "This has been quite a conversation. It feels like the door to my wisdom has opened up. I can hardly comprehend all the new insights I'm having. Could we talk in a couple of weeks?"

In our next call, Sharon excitedly reveals some of her new thoughts. "I'm bubbling over with enthusiasm since connecting with my inner coach. I haven't had a panic attack since you and I last spoke. I'm starting to see the distinction between fueling my panic-inducing thoughts, and feeding my well-being."

Sharon hesitates; then, after a few moments of quiet, carries on. "It's my choice, isn't it? I'm becoming more aware of the role of thought in creating my feelings; as a result, I'm more discerning. As for my innate health, my inner coach, if you will," she says humorously, "now I know it's inside me, I feel I can rely on it.

"I also realize," Sharon went on, "I hadn't really listened to my counselor. She was educating me on how thought works; thought flows, if we don't get so busy minded that we create a mental log-jam. But I didn't hear her. All I heard was the phrase 'feel the panic.' I focused on those specific words, bringing to life my fearful thoughts, to my own detriment.

"I do feel my counselor, in innocence, led me down the wrong path by even uttering those words. But I realize she was doing the best she could. I talked with her this morning, just before I called you, and told her how I was doing. She was delighted that I'm feeling good now, and was interested in what I've learned. I think she's heard something new as well. I've cancelled future appointments with her, both of us agreeing that it was no longer necessary for me to have therapy. I feel settled now. I know that I'm okay.

"I hope more people discover their inner coach, as I did. Wisdom will help them see the futility of encouraging negative feelings, and help them to realize they are heading in the wrong direction," Sharon said emphatically.

"I know everyone experiences a certain degree of pain in life. But we don't have to linger there, and we don't have to continue to bring up hurtful feelings in order to release them. I always thought not wanting to feel or acknowledge painful emotions was denial. Now I know it is not denial; it is wisdom," she said passionately. "It's up to us how we use the Principles to create our experience in life. I want to live in well-being," she ended decisively.

There is a big difference between ***seeing*** negative feelings, and feeling negative feelings. Wisdom provides the perspective to ***see*** negative thoughts without getting caught up in them.

Our inner coach, innate mental health, is buoyant, always waiting to be released. Acknowledge and appreciate this wonderful birthright, and solutions will appear to whatever needs to be addressed. We have the ability to "cook" our reality, to make our reality/experience real by our thoughts. As a wise friend said, "It's one thing to cook it; it's quite another thing to burn it to a crisp!"

"Laser Listening"

It's fascinating how the simplicity of the Principles can be confusing to people; yet, they will tell you they are enjoying themselves during the learning process. It appears to be a dichotomy. How can you enjoy yourself when you are confused?

When you think about it, it makes sense. Once you tap into your wisdom, you experience a sense of well-being, in addition to gaining inner knowledge. Wisdom, via a flash of insight, begins to reveal what the Principles are, and how they work. The intellect seems to move much slower than wisdom, hence the confusion. It takes time for the intellect to catch up with insight.

Let me give you an example. During a recent program for counselors who assist clients with career choices, I introduced the Three Principles. The workshop focused on the role of Thought in creating our view of life. We discussed how perception can affect one's career path. The second topic we explored was what I called "laser listening"—a deeper way of listening with a quiet, clear mind; being present in the moment.

The term, laser listening, occurred to me during intake with several of these career coaches. In order to be relevant to the group, I always like to check-in beforehand, to listen for what makes sense to them, and to see how I can connect their needs to the mystical principles of Mind, Consciousness and Thought.

As I listened, I discovered the participants had little or no understanding of the role of Thought in creating experience. I also heard how overworked they were—some counselors served up to ten clients a day. Occasionally, they would get attached to their clients' stories, and have a hard time staying uninvolved. The counselors were looking for new ways to impact their clients in a short time. Clearly, when you are overworked, tired and frustrated, your natural listening skills are not as keen as when you are operating from a state of well-being.

As I reflected on their needs, it was clear to me that if they could listen to their clients in a different way, in a way that would engage the clients' wisdom, they would have more impact. When you are in a quiet, clear, calm state of mind, the listening is laser like, and gets to the point quickly. In other words, you ***hear*** the heart, the essence of the clients' story, in a flash of clarity. Of course, the laser like quality of listening in a healthy state of mind works with whomever you are listening to, be it clients, family, friends, or yourself.

The coaches found it helpful when I shared with them that in a clear state of mind, you ***see*** the "innate mental health" in people. The problems they present are secondary. From this vantage point, you can direct your clients to their own wisdom. Their wisdom will calm them down so they can make better informed decisions, resolving their difficulties.

The workshop was a wonderful learning experience. The rapport among us deepened as we talked about the Principles. A mystical feeling swept over us, paving the way for deeper learning.

Some were very intrigued with the role of Thought in creating experience. They began to consider the power and relevance of this spiritual fact. I could see their faces light up as they began to engage their inner core of wisdom.

The participants found the principle of Consciousness to be hopeful, but some felt it was rather elusive. One coach said he was not sure if Consciousness would be practical. "However," he said thoughtfully, "I like the idea that Consciousness is our spiritual, impartial observer, always ready to guide us deeper into the source of wisdom. If

Consciousness really works that way, it definitely would be practical. I'll have to think about it," he mused.

I touched on the principle of Mind, our spiritual reservoir, where wisdom and insight occur. The fact that wisdom is inherent in people was a new thought for many, but seemed to appeal to them, and again, several were encouraged by this. Often, people tend to think wisdom is gained through age, experience, or education. Seldom do people see wisdom as intrinsic.

I introduced the idea of listening for that inner wisdom, as opposed to the more common psychological perspective of listening for what is troubling someone. The group educated me on the traditional methods of listening they had been taught; such as listening to your clients' problems, then reframing or redirecting them in a positive direction.

We discussed how reframing or redirecting doesn't address the root cause of people's problems: innocent unawareness of our true spiritual identity. As spiritual beings, we have the power to think, and to create our reality. This is where the role of Thought emerges and takes its place on the stage of life. When you discover you are the thinker, you begin to steer a wiser course, providing a much nicer existence. Yes, there are events in one's life that are thrust upon you. It's how you ***think*** about the event that makes the difference.

Susan, a counselor who works with physically challenged individuals, spoke up, "Elsie, I am getting the flavor of the role of Thought, and becoming more aware of its function, but we're going to need a lot of training to be able to do the laser listening with our clients."

In a flash I heard, "more aware of Thought." I asked Susan to consider the first part of her statement and forget the latter part. She paused for a moment, looked puzzled, and then ventured, "...more aware?"

"Yes, that's right! Where did the awareness of the role of Thought come from?"

She hesitated, and frowned, then her face cleared and she said, "Consciousness?"

"Exactly! Our consciousness is always aware, whether we realize it or not. All the Principles are functioning within us all the time. Why not use them as they are meant to be used—to make our life easier? Once we are pointed in the direction of our inner wisdom, we don't need a lot of training to laser listen, because we are learning through insight. In a manner of speaking, the Principles are our in-house trainer, and our in-house listener."

An attentive silence prevailed in the room. I knew they were hearing something; we rested comfortably in the momentary quiet. Then Susan exclaimed, "Elsie, you just did laser listening with me, didn't you?"

"That's right. And you "laser listened" to yourself—you listened from a deeper level, and heard something that sparked an insight! How long did that take?"

"About thirty seconds."

I felt an almost imperceptible shift in the group atmosphere. There was a buzz as comprehension started to dawn on the participants. We discussed how valuable it was for people to realize the Principles are inborn in everyone. Because the Principles are inherent, they are always available, to use as you wish. They are in service to you, particularly when you learn to cherish them as your birthright. This knowledge is an extraordinary thing to realize, and offers one great comfort.

Another coach verbalized his concern, "I don't know about this laser listening. It sounds too good to be true. Sometimes we don't have time to get quiet and calm. We have heavy schedules, and so little time."

"How long did the laser listening take with Susan?"

"Well, yes, you've got a point, but you're experienced."

"Experience can help, I agree, but it's not necessary. Susan's wisdom was sparked in a moment, and she is new to this understanding. That's the beauty of insight. It happens in a flash.

During the break, the group shared their thoughts with each other. Much discussion took place, and individuals were very attentive to each other. We gathered together again, and debriefed. Several people were visibly moved by their conversations.

Cheryl remarked, with a catch in her voice, "I had such a different dialogue with Lucas. We started off with how overworked we are, and how difficult our cases are. Then, somehow, our conversation shifted. I found myself hearing my friend's wisdom, in the midst of his describing his problems. It was really a different experience for me, but nice." A few people chuckled at Cheryl's comments.

Lucas responded, "I've never had anyone listen for my wisdom before, and I've certainly not listened to theirs either. It was so refreshing." Quite a few heads nodded in agreement.

Another counselor related, "I was standing by Jonas. We didn't really talk about much at first, and the quiet between us felt a little awkward. Then we relaxed with each other, and our conversation started to flow. I felt so at ease, so peaceful. I'm not usually comfortable in situations like this, but I felt Jonas was really interested in what I had to say."

Jonas inclined his head in agreement. "What I noticed is, I enjoyed listening to my co-worker. Normally," he said ruefully, "I admit I like being listened to—but I've not necessarily enjoyed listening to others. I've always wanted to get my opinion in first. I would listen to debate, convince, and seldom agree. This is the first time I've experienced a genuine enjoyment in simply listening. It's quite a novel experience." The room erupted with applause and laughter as Jonas struggled to be heard, "I can't wait to try this out with my clients."

The manager of the Career Coaches program, a man with a quiet demeanor, ended the session by acknowledging he felt this to be a transformational event. "It appears to me we are on track to offer more help to our clients. Understanding that the Three Principles reside within everyone affords new hope for being in service to our clients, colleagues, families, and ourselves. We can look at these Principles in a scientific manner, as well as an exploratory manner." He paused for a moment, and cleared his throat. "I believe it behooves us to also look at them with reverence."

Rapport – A Deeper Meaning of the Word

In the preceding chapter, we discussed the relationship between the Principles and listening deeply. We looked at wisdom and insight as gifts of Divine Mind. We pointed to the hopefulness and practicality of Consciousness, and the power of Thought we use in creating the human experience.

The chapter concluded with the manager of the program expressing his belief that the Three Principles could be looked at in a scientific way, and then stating, "It behooves us to also look at them with reverence."

Acknowledging the mystery and power of the Principles brings about a new depth of appreciation for the human spirit; we begin to see beyond people's behavior to the inner core of wisdom and mental health that we all share. From this perspective, judgment falls away and empathy prevails. We feel our connection with others, our human bond, and rapport happens effortlessly.

Often times, people think of rapport as a social connection, a result of people having certain beliefs or attitudes in common. What we are talking about here is a deeper meaning of the word; it comes from a feeling of oneness that is not dependent upon any outer conditions.

When this feeling is present, sensitive issues can be discussed with less likelihood of anyone getting defensive or insecure. If people do become insecure, a continued feeling of unconditional acceptance will help them calm down, allowing them space to listen attentively, and to hear more. Listening from a calm mind allows change to occur, because there is less distractive thinking.

Security is contagious. Speaking from a secure, compassionate state of mind clears the path for more meaningful communication. It engages people's innate wisdom. When people are operating from a healthy state of mind, there are practical and powerful results in the workplace, and in life.

Steve, a supervisor at a large electrical engineering firm, has had some difficulty communicating with his employees. He is from the old school of thought, where rapport is only possible if everyone is willing to participate. He feels that unless everyone is in agreement, rapport cannot be accomplished in a group setting.

Ramon, who manages the parts department, is a colleague of Steve's. Ramon sees that rapport (which he relates to a feeling of *camaraderie*) has great significance in the quality of interaction between management and employees. He understands that rapport, or the lack of it, also impacts work performance. During a coffee break, they have this conversation:

Ramon: "What do you mean when you say that rapport is dictated by others?"

Steve: "Well, you can't have open and honest communication in a meeting unless the rest of the group is willing. If they are hesitant to speak, or only have negative comments to make, it spoils it for the rest."

Ramon: "Yes, I can see this type of situation can make it more difficult. Still, I find if I remain open, curious, and really listen, the tone of the interaction can create a healthy dialogue that soon involves most everyone in the group."

Steve: "We tried team building awhile back, and when I brought up some sensitive issues about work performance, the employees got defensive. It's one thing to say, 'See the potential in people,' but what good does it do when they don't see it in themselves?"

Ramon: "Why do you think they got defensive?"

Steve: "We're cutting back and laying off some staff, so they see themselves as potential victims."

Ramon: "Being laid off is certainly a reason to feel uncertain about your future, but we're always going to have some uncertainty in our life. With all the cutbacks in the organization, I don't know if I'll have my job for much longer, either. What I do know is this: If we can see it's not the event that's stressing us, but our ***thinking*** about the event, this understanding will help a great deal."

Steve: "I've got two lines of thought on what you just said. We can see being laid off as an opportunity to find something better, or we can see ourselves as victims. When I said this to my employees, they got quite upset with me."

Ramon: "This type of situation is where I see rapport playing an important role. When you have deep rapport in place with your staff, when you genuinely see the potential in people, they will feel the compassion behind your words. The feeling of compassion will help keep them a little calmer. When people feel insecure, their behavior will reflect their insecurity. They are apt to be more pessimistic, and make challenging or negative statements. They certainly may feel apathetic toward their jobs. They might be feeling, 'What's the point if I'm being laid off?'"

Steve: "You would think that when someone is insecure about his job, he or she would perform better, in order to keep it."

Ramon: "I have rarely, if ever, seen insecurity lead to improved performance. A leader who ***sees*** the core potential in his employees will offer them an opportunity to change—from insecure people who see themselves as victims, to more confident individuals who see life as an opportunity."

Steve: "What do you mean? I don't have any other jobs to offer them."

Ramon: "I don't mean opportunity for another job. I mean an opportunity to change the way they see life. Simply by ***seeing*** beyond their insecure behavior, to their inner core, you offer them a chance to ***see*** themselves differently. When you don't buy into the negativity, it frees up mental space for you, and for your employees, so they can think more clearly.

Their wisdom is accessed, helping them through difficult times, as well as everyday situations.

"That is what rapport is all about. It is just another word for caring, for love. I know we don't talk about love in the workplace, but it's really the same thing. Let me put it another way. I've heard you talk about your grandchildren, and I know how much you care for them."

Steve: "What do my grandchildren have to do with anything?"

Ramon: "From what you've told me, you have a wonderful relationship with them. You listen to them and they listen to you, because of the love and rapport you share. Similarly, you and your employees will be more inclined to listen to each other when rapport is present. Rapport will help your employees listen with true attention, far more than when they are feeling intimidated and insecure."

Steve: "It's not the same thing. These people are my employees, not my grandchildren."

Ramon: "Even so, rapport works the same with everyone. Deep rapport allows sensitive information to be shared, without people getting so defensive. If they do get defensive, and you maintain your level of calmness and caring, chances are they will be more likely to see it as just information, and not be so gripped by the outcome. This will help them transition in their lives, and be more comfortable with seeing what they need to do, what other career opportunities are available."

Steve: "But—"

Ramon: "Before you disagree, Steve, hold on a second and look at the conversation we're having right now. We've shared some sensitive issues, and there has been very little push back, wouldn't you agree?"

Steve: "That's true. I've questioned you, but I haven't felt upset, just curious about your ideas. You seem pretty confident and adamant, and I can feel that what you're saying is coming from a genuine desire to help. I'll definitely give it some thought, Ramon. I know I would like to have a deeper connection to my employees, and to be in service to them during this crucial period."

Ramon: "Wanting to be in service shows that you truly care about them, and are on the way to developing the deep rapport we've been talking about. Seeing the wisdom and unlimited potential in people, even when they're not seeing it themselves, is like a magic ingredient that brings out natural intuition, new enjoyment and satisfaction with life. And it affects everyone involved, not just the employees."

Steve: "All right, buddy. I get the message!"

Tight Pants Syndrome

Have you ever felt a bit of a letdown after the holiday festivities? Enjoying our family, friends, the giving and receiving of gifts, all the wonderful food—sometimes it takes a while to get back to "normal." Perhaps our clothes are feeling a bit snug and slightly uncomfortable.

We make New Year's resolutions to lose weight, exercise more, eat healthier, stop smoking, be more organized, become more patient and more appreciative of what we have. Turning over a new leaf seems like a refreshing idea and we are motivated to move ahead, diligently adhering to our decision to make changes. We begin eating better, and soon we feel slimmer and healthier. We are full of gratitude as we accomplish much of our "to do" list.

So why do old habits sneak up on us? Sometimes it feels that just as we are doing so well, old habits of thinking and habits of action reappear in our life. Pretty soon, we may experience the "tight pants syndrome" where we, once again, are feeling uncomfortable with the fit of our pants, or the fit of our old habits. We may not feel on top of our game.

The "tight pants syndrome" is a metaphor for an individual trying on habits of thought from the past, finding them uncomfortable; yet at the same time finding it difficult to let them go. The habits are familiar to us, as are the pants; after all, we've had them for a long time. They used to be quite comfortable, so what has happened? We've gained weight? We've gained knowledge? Could that be why our old habits are so uncomfortable now, because we know more? Is it because we've opened more to our True Self?

True knowledge is a wonderful gift, a gift for all seasons. If we see this time of transition as a learning experience, and don't judge ourselves harshly, we can move forward with a fair amount of ease. If we judge ourselves or others, this judgment can lead to blame, resentment, and frustration, adding a lot of needless stress. Now is the time to count on our inner resources and trust that our wisdom will come through.

Cheryl is experiencing the "tight pants syndrome." Although she has had some education in the Three Principles, Cheryl has gained more of an intellectual understanding than insight. She is aware of her stress, but oblivious to the fact that her negative thoughts are contributing to her angst. Unaware of her inner process, Cheryl is struggling to understand why, lately, her life seems to have gone from smooth sailing to stormy seas. "If every cloud has a silver lining," she wonders, "Why is it pouring on me?" She is trying to rise above her low mood, but finds herself impatient in her interactions with co-workers. She takes everything personally, and feels frustrated, thinking that her teammates are out to get her. She decides to talk with Jeff, the Employee Assistance Counselor at her organization.

Cheryl explains what she is feeling. "I've noticed that I'm gripped by what is going on around me, so I'm saying very little in the meetings. It seems that every time I open my mouth, I am challenged by one of my team. Consequently, I feel it is better that I say nothing.

"Not all the team members have had training in the Three Principles approach," Cheryl continues, "so they don't understand the value of this knowledge. I do the best I can to share with them what I've learned, but they make disparaging remarks like, "State of mind has nothing to do with producing widgets." So I feel it's best to keep my thoughts to myself, watch my body language, and try to remain calm," she concluded.

Jeff listened attentively and said nothing for a time. He waited for insight into Cheryl's situation. Presently, he said,

"Did you know that challenging statements are often driven by insecurity and lack of understanding?"

"Well, I do remember learning something about insecurity in my training on the Three Principles, but to be honest, I've forgotten it," Cheryl responded. "Is it important?"

"It's insecurity that drives ego behavior," Jeff stated, "and insecurity is thought. We have the power to create insecure behavior by thinking insecure thoughts. Understanding how thought works is helpful. Even more valuable is gaining insight into the true nature of Thought. As you learn more about the nature of the Principles, you engage your wisdom, which automatically diminishes judgment and relieves frustration.

"True knowledge brings compassion for those who are struggling with insecurity, including compassion for yourself," Jeff said softly. "Take a step back and see there is much personal development going on inside you. Be grateful for this opportunity, instead of distressed. I know sometimes this is difficult to understand, and it feels hard to do—but the instant you ***see*** beyond behavior, the ***seeing*** brings great relief and clarity."

"I know I should be grateful for what I've learned from the Principles training. I should try to remain calm and not take personally the things they say. But I don't see how on earth I can appreciate being ignored by my team and—"

Jeff gently interrupted, "The more you ***see*** the nature of Thought, rather than the resulting behavior of insecure thought, the less personally you will take things. Then you will ***be*** calm, not "try" to be calm, and you won't have to watch your body language. You will be relaxed and at ease, observing those around you with understanding and compassion."

Jeff paused for a moment, then with a thoughtful look in his eye, said, "Your team mates just don't see that state of mind has everything to do with producing widgets. Your colleagues are not out to get you or to deliberately antagonize you, although it may seem that way. They are simply reacting from how they perceive life. In their minds, they really don't see the connection between state of mind and life in general. They are psychologically innocent, given how they think."

There was a long drawn out sigh from Cheryl. "I hear what you are saying, Jeff, and it does make sense to me. I just don't understand why I'm falling into old habits again, like taking things personally. I thought I knew better, and yet here I am doing the same things I did before."

"Don't be so hard on yourself, Cheryl. I think you've got a lot of courage coming to see me to learn more about life. Take credit for your commitment to living in a healthy state of mind.

"As for why we re-visit old habits, I would say it is just the way we learn. Often times, revisiting old patterns of behavior feels worse now because we do know better. I call this process 'tight pants syndrome'...because old habits feel tight and uncomfortable, just as old pants can. When we have an honest look at this process, we realize that we've outgrown our habits; this realization allows clarity to emerge. It's like we get to breathe freely again. Our habits aren't constricting us and we are breathing the fresh air of new knowledge."

There was a long pause while Cheryl absorbed this information. "I did my best not to take the team's comments to heart. That's why I just kept quiet during the meeting," Cheryl said, as she shifted restlessly in her chair.

"Did you feel quiet inside yourself? Or were you just being quiet verbally?"

"Hmm, good question, Jeff. Actually, when I think of it, I felt ticked off at the team because I've tried so hard to be in service to them," and with her tone rising, Cheryl said, "and this is what I get back—abuse and disrespect!"

"Now we're getting down to it," Jeff chuckled. "It's good to be honest about your feelings, so long as you don't continue to fan the flame of negative emotions. We all feel aggravated from time to time. There is nothing wrong with that. It's part of the human experience. When we take these feelings as real, and not as thoughts in action, then we can do damage to others and ourselves. Honesty clears the air so our consciousness can rise to the surface and guide us to more understanding."

"Something just occurred to me, Jeff," Cheryl exclaimed excitedly. "Listening with compassion, and being quiet with understanding, is very different from not saying anything while judgmental thoughts are going on inside my mind. I was being insecure as well. My judgment was being motivated by my insecure thoughts. I didn't realize what I was doing until just now. I can't wait to get back to work and talk with the team again."

A couple of months went by before Jeff and Cheryl's next meeting. "I can't believe how different I feel, Jeff. After our last conversation about the nature of the Principles, I found myself ***seeing*** the Principles with more clarity. This has helped me discern that Thought is an innate, neutral power that we are meant to use with wisdom. I never knew we had the gift to create a life so satisfying and filled with contentment. I feel jubilant, relieved and grateful.

"In our team meetings, I find myself listening with curiosity, with more neutrality, and much less judgment. I had to laugh at myself when I remembered I had told you I didn't take to heart the sentiments my team expressed. Now I do take their comments to heart, in a healthy way. I'm able to hear the remarks that are insecurity driven, without taking them personally. I understand that insecure comments are best defused by compassion. I'm now able to be in service in a way that wasn't possible before, when I was so reactive, and I take care of what needs to be done with a sense of satisfaction.

"This understanding is powerful," Cheryl continued, "and has far reaching impact. Most of the team is responding in a positive manner. Living what I've learned about the Three Principles is having much more influence on the team than trying to share verbally what I've learned. It appears that the old adage of 'walk your talk' has merit.

"Jeff, I really appreciate what you've taught me. You talked about the 'tight pants syndrome' of old habits. I feel like I've shed a lot of my old habits and found a new attitude toward life. That's better than new pants, or a whole new wardrobe!"

Living in the Past

The subtlety of living in the past has taken on new meaning for me. I used to think living in the past meant bringing up bad memories and using them to hurt yourself or others. I didn't realize that good memories can also get in the way of seeing "what is" now.

Let me give you an example. In 2006 we decided to downsize, sell our large ocean-view home, and simplify our life style. Without realizing it, I had expectations our home would sell in a very short time. The previous times we had come to a major life decision that included a move, our home had sold within a week. So I automatically assumed the same thing would happen again.

I went about the business of listing our home, and started to consider what items we should sell, give away, or keep. I actually started to pack some items, so as to be ready to move at a moment's notice.

As the first month went by and our home didn't sell, I began to get edgy, wondering what the problem was. Granted, we had listed in October, toward the end of the busy real estate selling time, but we had listed in October with previous homes and sold very quickly. The thought crossed my mind that perhaps our realtor wasn't doing enough to move our property. I discussed this with Ken, and he suggested that I "sit tight," and wait to see how things progressed. This is typical of Ken, not to make waves, and I held my tongue. Nonetheless, I decided to give our realtor a call.

The next day, while I was in a low mood, I called our agent to take him to task for not selling our home as I expected. I began to build a case in my mind to substantiate my rationale that he wasn't doing a good job. I ruminated on my earlier experiences with realtors who had sold our properties rapidly. I had a head of steam up when I called our agent. Fortunately, he was unavailable. Leaving a message, I went for a walk down to the ocean near our home. Sitting on a log, contemplating the seagulls fishing, smelling the ocean breeze, brought calmness to my mind.

I realized that the situation didn't really have anything to do with our realtor. He was doing all he could to sell our property. The market simply wasn't buying at the time. My low mood wasn't about the event of selling our home. It became evident to me that my faulty ***thinking*** about the event created my low mood.

In a low state of mind, I had come to resent our house, feeling it was a big elephant that was difficult to sell. I had stopped noticing the beauty of our surroundings, and the magnificent ocean view. All I saw was what was wrong with it; that it was a huge dwelling with too much to clean and maintain.

In a calm state of mind, I saw not only our house, but also our realtor with different eyes. When I did eventually speak with him, he was kind, unruffled, and unperturbed by my questions as to why our home wasn't selling. He calmly offered his reasons, which were absolutely valid, and we were able to have a healthy and productive conversation. We came to a satisfactory agreement on what we could do to move things along.

The shift in my perspective allowed me to relax, be patient, and continue to enjoy our home. I admired the beautiful sea vista, with every description of boat sailing by, and the white shell beach on the small island, visible in the distance. How lucky we are, I thought, to live in this stunningly beautiful residence.

With fresh eyes, I was able to ***see*** and be so grateful to Ken for his level of understanding while I struggled with my impatience and judgment of others. He was steadfast in moving forward with whatever needed to be done. He continued to putter in his workshop, and to live his life as if there was no move planned. Of course, there were moments when he also became edgy, but on the whole, his ability to be in the moment with whatever was going on was a blessing.

Because the decision to downsize and simplify our life had been based on insight, I again assumed that everything would fall into place immediately. The understanding that I ultimately came to is this. The insight showed us the pathway to follow. The timing of the path unfolding is unknown. Learning as we travel the trail is part of the journey, and to relax and enjoy it is part of the journey. Travelling so rapidly that you lose sight of the beauty around you certainly defies logic and is not wise. I am exceedingly appreciative to have learned more about following the pathway, not based on my sense of time, but trusting the timelessness of the what is meant to be.

Here's another example of innocently living in the past. One day during a call with a client, Roseanne, she mentioned a situation she was struggling with regarding her annual management performance assessment.

"I'm not real happy with my supervisor's assessment of my overall performance," Roseanne told me, "and I was wondering if you could give me some tips.

"I was rated a 3 out of 5," she continued, "which means I met expectations but have room for improvements. I feel I rate a 4, and I have prepared a rebuttal for my supervisor, outlining the merits of my performance and defending my position in other areas."

Roseanne continued to spell out her grievances. I could hear her getting more defensive as she related her story. She was unknowingly blaming everyone else for her performance and couldn't seem to see her own role. One of the things she mentioned was that her supervisor felt she was living in the past, in terms of making management decisions.

The supervisor's comment really seemed to tick Roseanne off. "I take exception to that point," she said in an angry tone. "I feel if a certain policy or procedure is working, why fix what isn't broken? Some of the staff tell me there are better ways to do things, more current ideas, but I don't agree with them. After all, I've been a manager with this company for thirty years, and the new team leaders haven't been here as long. Obviously, they don't know all the 'ins and outs' of why we do things in a certain way."

"It's an interesting situation, Roseanne. You know my coaching approach is not to get into the details of your situation, but it would be helpful for me to hear what 'living in the past' means to you?"

"I don't know what you mean, and I don't understand what my supervisor is getting at either. I don't live in the past. I come in to work every morning feeling it's a new day."

I asked Roseanne if it would be helpful to her if I shared what living in the past meant to me, and to share an example. She said, "Go ahead. I'd like to hear your story."

I related what I was learning from my experience of selling our home, and how I'd discovered I was living in the past of good memories. "Those memories led to expectations which got in my way of seeing life as it is now," I stated. "Living in the past prevented me from living in the present."

Roseanne listened attentively and I thought, "Great, she's really getting it."

"I wouldn't have done what you did, Elsie. I can see you were living in the past, but I don't live like that."

I must admit I was a little taken aback at my client's statement. "Well, I've been put in my place," I thought. Then the innocence of her remark struck my funny bone, as I realized Roseanne couldn't see that she also was living in the past. Adhering to the same management decisions she'd made many years ago, that were now no longer as effective, kept her locked in a time capsule.

Roseanne spoke again. "The only thing that comes to my mind when you ask what living in the past means is that it's a red herring."

"A red herring?" I asked with astonishment. "What do you mean by that?"

"I mean that people may say 'You're living in the past', about my decision to continue using the same procedures we've used for thirty years as a means of deflecting attention from their own issues."

"I see," I said slowly. "I never thought of it like that. Perhaps in some cases that may be so. At the beginning of our call, you asked me for some tips. What if, in this instance, we took a fresh look at how your performance assessment is an opportunity for change—perhaps to build healthier relationships, to be open to new ideas, and to listen to others with more attention? Don't you think it would be worth it; to see how to enhance your leadership performance?"

"I really don't see what you're getting at, Elsie. I don't bring the past into the new day," Roseanne insisted.

Silence stretched out over the phone.

"Maybe subconsciously, but not consciously," Roseanne reluctantly acknowledged.

"You've hit the nail on the head, Roseanne," I responded enthusiastically. "That's exactly right. I certainly wasn't aware that I was living in the past when I was getting upset about our house not selling. Psychologically, I was unaware of what I was doing until I had a moment of quiet insight and realized what was happening. The realization completely changed my perspective.

"Often, we are unaware of how much we are living in the past. We may see the tip of the iceberg, but the greater part is hidden, until insight brings it to light."

"I'll have to think about that," replied Roseanne, in a hesitant tone. It appeared she had enough food for thought. We agreed to table the discussion for the moment and talk again in a month's time. I had the feeling that Roseanne's psychological defense system had been shaken, in a positive way. Her mind was aerated, which would allow new insights to emerge. The power of insight would help move her beyond the past, into the present.

Red Herring Stories

A month went by quickly, and soon it was time to speak with Roseanne. I was eager to see if my client had gained insight about moving beyond the past. As it turned out, we didn't speak about that at all, at least not at the beginning of our conversation.

Our discussion centered on how Roseanne could build healthier relationships with her team. She felt this would act as a catalyst for moving the department ahead. I could see that, as the manager, she had a genuine commitment to helping her team develop to meet, and possibly exceed, their department goals.

I asked her what she thought got in the way of the team coalescing. She pondered this for a moment; then responded, "People are reluctant to let their guard down to discuss issues, or to ask how to do better."

"What do you think would help them get past their reluctance?"

"I don't know." She then proceeded to tell me a lengthy story about something else altogether. I had noticed that when asked a direct question, Roseanne would often circumvent the inquiry with a story that really had nothing to do with the issue.

Once again I queried her, "What do you think would help your team get past their reluctance to discuss relevant issues?"

Roseanne proceeded to tell yet another story. "Excuse me," I interrupted. "I don't mean to be rude, but do you see that you are going off track and not answering my question? You said other people do this to distract attention from the issues. You called it a 'red herring.' Do you remember saying that in our last conversation, when I asked you what living in the past meant to you?"

There was a long silence, and then another story came. I smiled as I asked, "Roseanne, would you rather we didn't pursue this subject?"

"No, no. That's quite all right. I was just thinking. Go ahead and ask me again."

"Let me ask you the same question in another way. How do you think you might help your team feel safer, so they would feel free to contribute their ideas?"

"What do you mean 'feel safer'?"

"I mean providing a mentally healthy environment, where people are listened to and encouraged to share their opinions."

"I do that already. I sent them all an email asking them for their ideas, and no one responded."

"I see. May I ask if you followed up your email and talked to them personally?"

"No, I didn't. I felt they should have responded to my email."

"It would have been great if they had replied," I agreed. "As the leader, you may need to take the initiative and move forward, rather than waiting for your people to get back to you. Approaching them would strengthen relationships, which is what you said you wanted to do. It's clear to me that you have the team's welfare at heart. I don't think it would take much to get the group involved in a way that would promote more interest and cooperation."

There was a lengthy pause. "Now that you mention it," Roseanne said, nodding her head thoughtfully, "it seems like a good idea."

Roseanne went on to say that she was aware she needed to move forward with the team development plan, and to stay focused on their goals and objectives. She added, "Now that I'm aware it would be a good idea to follow-up on the email to my team, I will do so. I never thought it was up to me until you mentioned it. I thought if my staff was interested, it was up to them to contact me. When they didn't, I assumed they were indifferent."

A light went on for me when she mentioned the word "aware" again. It occurred to me to ask her what she understood about how we create our reality. She pondered this for some time. "By being aware of choices."

"Say more about that, Roseanne. That's a very interesting comment."

"It's deciding which thought to follow, being aware of reaction, and choosing not to go there. For example, the other day in a conversation I was having with a colleague, I felt the conversation was getting a bit heated. I felt upset, so I didn't pursue the subject. I chose not to go down that path."

"That's great, Roseanne. Well done."

"I learned long ago, once you get mad, you've lost the argument."

"That's a very wise statement," I approved.

"Can I ask you another question, Roseanne?" She agreed. "Do you see that the heightened awareness you experienced is the principle of Consciousness in action?"

She considered my question, and then responded, "No, I didn't realize that. I've never thought much about Consciousness."

"Yet you pepper your conversation with the word 'aware.' Consciousness, or awareness, as you refer to it, plays an important role in creating our experience. Mind, Consciousness and Thought work in partnership to create our personal reality. In your words, 'Being aware of choices' is like being aware of thoughts, and which thoughts to focus on to form a better reality."

"What?" she asked, uncomprehendingly.

I burst out laughing, realizing I had gone too far, and soon she joined me. "Not to worry, Roseanne. You already are making better choices because you are more aware. You've got it!"

As we were wrapping up our conversation, Roseanne said, "I will pay close attention to the 'red herring' stories I tell. I didn't realize I was avoiding the issue by telling these stories. I thought it was a way to share what I knew without being too direct with my team. I see now that it gets in the way of pursuing the topic in question, and people stop listening. I honestly thought I was giving them a valuable lesson. Experiences are a wonderful thing to share, but we need to use them at the proper time. Now that I know this, I feel I can be more direct, and listen with respect and openness."

After a period of comfortable silence, she mused, "It's just dawning on me now that when I'm dodging the issue, I am operating in the past, because I am not listening ***now***. I never realized that before. When you talked about living in the past, I thought you meant living in past memories, and I didn't think I did that. Now I see that when I'm telling stories from the past, I'm actually living in the past."

"It depends on the ***feeling*** that is attached to the story, Roseanne. If the feeling is positive and vital, there is nothing wrong with telling stories from the past. We all do that. However, it's important to be sensitive to the feeling of the situation. If the feeling isn't constructive, and the people you're talking with aren't attentive, take that as a sign that the story isn't having impact. Pause for a moment to listen to your wisdom and common sense. Listening will tell you the appropriate action to take at that time.

"When you paused a moment ago, you had the insight about living in the past. In other words, you paused and listened to your own wisdom. Insights only occur when you are present in the moment."

Such a strong feeling of understanding flowed between us that additional words were unnecessary. The silent rapport spoke volumes more than mere words could convey.

Finally I said, "Roseanne, you've made my day! What you have discovered just now is very insightful, and will help you develop healthier relationships at all levels of your organization, as well as in your personal life."

Roseanne gave a carefree laugh and said, "I'll hold you to that."

I was delighted with what Roseanne had shared with me. Realizing that her "red herring stories" were getting in the way of open, honest communication with her team, and with others in the organization, was a significant step in her inner development. Her insightful discovery about living in the past had taken her to a deeper level of understanding, a deeper level of Consciousness. I was honored and gratified to have travelled on the pathway with her.

Incremental Change

Sometimes, when people are experiencing a rough patch in their lives, they think that they haven't learned much at all. Everything they see is colored by this state of mind. They may find themselves being judgmental, frustrated, stressed, and feeling negative in general.

Often, people will tell me they are disappointed that they have fallen back into an unhealthy state of mind. They assumed that once they had experienced healthy functioning, they would always operate in that mode. They find difficulty accepting a shift into lower levels of consciousness, and blame themselves for not maintaining their well-being. Of course, this mental attitude just exacerbates the situation. At that moment in time, they are not grateful for having had some insight that changed their life; they are not appreciative of incremental change.

Understanding that life is an on-going process of gaining more knowledge about the nature of our True Identity, and the nature of the Principles, is a crucial point in our inner development. This awareness deters us from lingering in a state of frustration and judgment. ***Seeing*** a lower state of mind with neutrality immediately shifts us to a higher level of learning and functioning.

When driving a vehicle, we know to slow down when we come to a rough patch in the road, in order to navigate safely. As we learn to see the benefits of quieting down our personal thinking when we hit the inevitable "bumps" along the road of life, it makes navigation of our mental terrain much easier.

What are the benefits of slowing down? There is less cyclical thinking, and more clarity with which to view the situation. This clarity lessens judgment, stress, and gives us more mental traction to move forward. It also brings deeper feelings of gratitude for what we have learned.

So often, people think that change constitutes a dramatic turn-around in one's life. That does happen, but not all the time. Much of the time, the changes we experience are incremental. In the business world, the term is "step-level" change. We gain knowledge, a little at a time; or occasionally, a lot at a time. The trick is to be grateful for any change, large or small. It's all good!

Incremental change can be a moment of quiet in a person you may think isn't hearing anything. The moment of calm is that individual's ego pausing, perhaps for a split second, and wisdom coming to the forefront. The person's intellect may take over again, but that moment of quiet is step-level change.

Another example of incremental change is when someone who would never admit to making a mistake acknowledges an error. That increased awareness is a shift in consciousness that is life changing, and will surely affect those around him or her. Seeing incremental change also helps us be less intense in our desire to see things change rapidly. We trust that life has a way of unfolding in the most appropriate and timely manner.

It is a great service to point out incremental change to someone who is psychologically struggling. It helps them see themselves and others with a less jaundiced view. An individual who is mentally agitated may not realize that he has changed; that he is more open to conversation, not as angry, not as withdrawn as he was a year ago. When this is pointed out to him, he is more apt to listen, and to gently ease out of his distress.

Here is an illustration. Darren's mind is filled with thoughts of judgment, and consequently, he feels angry and frustrated. He is upset at being required to support what he sees as poor policy coming from upper management. Darren doesn't have judgment about the person who made the decision; he just has judgment about the program.

Darren's lack of judgment about the decision maker is step-level change in his psychological understanding. A year ago, Darren would have thought his boss was a big jerk for making, in his mind, a poor decision. Now, he sees that his boss is doing the best he can, given how he (the boss) sees life. When this fact was brought to Darren's attention, he couldn't see the significance at first. He was exasperated at himself for not being able to let go of his frustration, and was feeling a good deal of angst.

The moment Darren realized the mental change he had experienced over the last year, his state of mind shifted into higher gear. He saw new options on how he could communicate with his boss, and perhaps, come to a better understanding of why the executive decision was made.

At the very least, Darren could accept that there wasn't anything he could do at this point, other than keep his well-being as best he could, and come to terms with the announcement. Often times, when acceptance comes into the picture, it clears our mind and we begin to see ways we may help alter or improve the situation. Failing that, we can remain in service the best we can, under the circumstances.

For example, Darren was able to help his team come to grips with the questionable edict from upper management. There had been a great deal of confusion amongst the employees because of the turnabout on what the company was going to do. Morale took a dip south; grumbling ensued, rumors pervaded the department, and the overall tone was not conducive to healthy, productive communication, support for each other, or support for the company.

As Darren regained his healthy state of mind, he observed the low morale. Instead of contributing to it, as he had been doing, he was able to share a fresh perspective on the situation. This helped the team settle down and regain their footing. Morale improved, and although I'd like to say the story ends like a fairy tale, the reality is, the decision still appears to have been a poor one.

However, since morale has improved, the employees are not up in arms about it. They are seeing the event with a fair amount of equilibrium. Darren and his team have shifted their perspective to seeing what upper management is doing right, rather than focusing on what they have done wrong.

The shift of focus has had enormous consequences. It has cleared the deck for improved communication at all levels. Darren is engaging his team in highly productive, creative dialogues about accomplishing the mission of the company. The team is experiencing higher levels of job satisfaction, there is reduced tardiness and absenteeism; the team is having fun!

Other employees are noticing the healthy tone of this group, and are curious and interested in the change of this particular department. Although there are some who say, "It won't last," the point is hardly debatable. A healthy, positive tone in an organization has a way of catching on. The overriding result is that employees in general become more self-motivated and self-directed. They **own** their jobs with pride and satisfaction.

Incremental change—sounds like not much happens until you take a moment to really see that step-level change indicates a shift in consciousness, leading to more personal and professional development. Again, "It's all good!"

The "Blips" of Life

In the last chapter, "Incremental Change", we looked at how we may judge others, and ourselves, when we are experiencing a bumpy ride in life. We explored how change in an individual can affect others in an organization. In this chapter, we will look at how change in an individual can affect personal relationships, and perhaps, create some "blips" along the way.

Murray is in love! Everything is rosy and life has never looked better. Murray and his girlfriend, Anne, met at a Three Principles seminar. Murray was very taken with the philosophy, and Anne, although she considered it an interesting approach, continued her search for other knowledge.

They have been dating for a year, and have come to realize they are meant for one another. They feel their love is deep and abiding, and discover nuances in their relationship that they've never experienced with anyone else. Truly, they feel blessed.

Now, we move ahead through time. Murray and Anne have been married for two years, and their relationship, although still solid and strong, is experiencing some growing pains. They don't always agree with each other, or understand the other's point of view.

Murray has had a long-held habit of withdrawing when things get edgy, whereas Anne has always liked to dig in and get to the bottom of the matter. When Murray withdraws, Anne feels he's not being attentive to their relationship. When Anne presses on to find out what is bothering Murray, he feels she is being pushy. They appear to be at a stalemate.

What is so interesting in this situation is that when Murray withdraws, it looks to him as if he is just repeating his old habit. Because he is not thinking clearly, he feels guilty about this. The worse he feels, the more his thinking becomes entrenched. His tendency to extricate himself from possible conflict doesn't look constructive to him, and he ruminates on how best to deal with this.

However, what Murray hasn't fully grasped is that he has shifted in his level of consciousness, and hasn't quite caught up with that shift yet. What he has learned about creating the human experience has given him a different perspective, almost despite himself.

When Murray drew back in the past, it was because he always wanted to please people, to keep their approval, so he wouldn't stand up for himself with respect and dignity. Now, with common sense in place, his withdrawal from negativity is guided by wisdom, not habit. Clearly, it is best to wait until the tone is positive before discussing sensitive issues.

Fortunately, Murray soon becomes tired of his mental calisthenics and relaxes. As his mind stills, Murray realizes that disengaging from negativity is productive! His insight creates an open and safe mental environment in which the couple can reflect, and listen to one another without their old habits getting in the way. They begin to see how consciousness informs the intellect, which helps them resolve their different approaches to communicating with each other. Another "blip" is smoothed out, and harmony reigns once again in their household.

Incremental change in an individual and the impact on relationships can appear subtle. We may not even be aware of the fact that we've changed. It bears repeating: It often takes time for our intellect to catch up with our insights. When we find ourselves gripped by old patterns of thought, it may seem as if the insights we've gained have disappeared. We may feel as if our wisdom doesn't work for us any longer; that wisdom has taken a holiday, and apparently, forgotten to return. We may wonder if the Three Principles really apply in every situation we face in life.

Not to worry! The "blips" of life provide a classroom to further our education. In a classroom where we learn the principles of mathematics, we learn first how to add, subtract, divide and multiply. Then we may move on to calculus, physics, and so on. We continue to learn and grow in our understanding of calculation.

In the same way, as we delve deeper into the mystery of who and what we really are, our understanding of how we function and create personal reality is enhanced. Our comprehension continues to grow as we experience diverse and varied situations; some are challenging, some easy, some unpleasant, some fascinating, and some we may never want to experience again.

If we open up to feelings of curiosity and gratitude, regardless of whether or not we see the purpose of whatever experience we are having, these deeper feelings can help neutralize any drama that may occur. You might think this is not possible in the case of severe trauma or physical violence. But what if it is? Consider the healing this understanding offers those who experience such trauma. I ask that you reserve judgment and read on.

It makes a world of difference to whether we take on stress, or discern the deeper purpose of wisdom, when we experience learning with curiosity and gratitude. Let me clarify what I mean by this. Consider curiosity in the sense of wonder, having a glimmer of our true spiritual nature. Consider curiosity as neutral, as patience, knowing that the answer for "why" will come, knowing that wisdom will manifest, given an opening.

Gratitude for the "blips" of life may seem a difficult feeling to achieve. The feeling of gratitude isn't achieved—the quality of gratitude I'm pointing to is released or uncovered. There are different feelings of gratitude. Some may think gratitude is a feeling of "Wow, isn't this great!" And that feeling certainly occurs. However, the feeling of gratitude implied in this chapter is more a feeling of calm acceptance, a deeper feeling of reflection on what can be learned from any life situation.

Lynda's husband, Shawn, is a cancer survivor. He has had several bouts of chemotherapy, and the cancerous tumors seemed to be in remission. When he had his last examination, the doctors discovered two more tumors and removed them. Lynda and Shawn were deeply discouraged because they thought the cancer had been vanquished.

That evening in the hospital, they both sought to support each other by trying to be positive, but the "trying" wasn't very successful. Shawn was quiet and withdrawn. Lynda left at the close of visiting hours and returned home, spending a sleepless night.

When Lynda arrived at the hospital the next morning, she couldn't believe her eyes. Her husband was in good spirits and ready to go home! Shawn told her that he realized it was a wonderful thing to have only two tumors removed this time, rather than the several he had had removed many times before. He felt the removal of two tumors was incremental change, and that meant his physical health was improving. His spirit was so light-hearted and genuine; he was not denying that he had cancer, but he was thankful it wasn't any worse.

Lynda was very moved by her husband's wisdom, and felt a shift in her own state of mind as well. They were no longer "trying" to be positive. They were truly functioning from a feeling of gratefulness. Shawn told his wife, "If anyone had told me a year ago that I would be grateful for two tumors, I would have said they were crazy! I'm just so glad to be alive."

The situation was definitely a "blip" on life's radar screen, but rather than continuing to struggle with it, both Shawn and Lynda accepted "what is" with grace and equanimity.

At the same time, Shawn followed his own good judgment, taking whatever homeopathic supplements it made sense to take, in addition to the traditional treatment. Common sense and wisdom prevailed, supporting and sustaining the couple.

If we can see the anomalies of life from this wise perspective, it will make the path on our journey a great deal smoother, far less stressful, and much more enjoyable. One of the signposts on the path is **"Gratitude Paves the Way"**.

Supersize Wisdom

We live in a fast paced world, with everything at our fingertips. Broadband access brings the Internet to us in an instant. We can connect with information anywhere in the world. It can be a wonderful gift, but sometimes it can be information overload, leading to information indigestion. Sometimes I feel that we need an information diet!

Fast food restaurants offer to "supersize" our portion for mere pennies, so it seems we can't pass up the deal. We're inundated with instant gratification opportunities. Society seems to gravitate toward supersizing everything we can. Supersizing becomes a habit, supported by the world around us. How can we help it then, when we want to supersize our wisdom? And not only supersize wisdom, but supersize it NOW!

It's an interesting predicament we have gotten ourselves into, innocently to be sure. Nonetheless, the instant gratification attitude can be a barrier to allowing our innate wisdom to emerge. Not satisfied with spontaneously gaining insight into what the mind is and how it works, we "try" to acquire more self-awareness. What a blessing to comprehend that being thankful for the insightful knowledge we find is the path to releasing more.

Josh is the business manager for a small but busy graphic design firm. Not only does he manage the business, but he is also a very talented graphic artist who contributes a great deal to the development and implementation of various projects. He never seems to catch up with his work, and often pulls "all-nighters" to complete his assignments. Deep down, he doesn't like the way his life is; he doesn't have time for his family or for himself.

Josh knows that when he's calm, he's more clearheaded, his creativity is activated, and he produces more work in a shorter period of time. But this state of calm seems to elude him for long intervals. It whispers to him from time to time, so he knows it's still there—but how to maintain this state of mind more of the time? Josh tells me he doesn't have time to be calm! He wishes he could supersize his hours in order to manage his work more effectively.

Alma is a caseworker for a social service agency, providing services for victims of natural disasters. She is a caring and conscientious person, who puts her heart and soul into her work. Alma often finds herself overwhelmed with her job, trying to meet all the demands on her time, and on her ability to provide the services that are needed. She becomes short tempered, snaps at her co-workers, has difficulty sustaining a civil relationship with her supervisor, and her home life is giving her grief.

Alma attends a Three Principles course, recommended by her supervisor. She is a bit resistant at first. She regrets the hours she is required to put in at the training, because it takes away from the time she has to accomplish her duties at work. However, the training is lighthearted and the tone is upbeat, so Alma finds herself relaxing, and reluctantly enjoying herself. At one point, the instructor, Denise, talks about the value of calmness in maintaining a healthy tone when interacting with clients and co-workers, and Alma is compelled to speak.

"I like what you are saying," she tells Denise, "and I'd like to believe you. But I just don't have the time to be calm at the office. There is no way I can sit quietly in my chair, meditate for five minutes, and then go back to work. It just doesn't make sense. I need calmness now," she declared adamantly, "and I need lots of it!"

Denise smiles, "So you want to supersize calmness, and you want it now. Okay, let's see what we can do about that.

Let's take this one step at a time. Did I say anything about sitting quietly in your chair and meditating?"

"No, you didn't, but that's what it sounds like I would have to do, to be calm," she states vigorously.

Denise walks closer to Alma and holds her gaze. "Alma, I want you to listen carefully to what I am going to say. Calmness isn't about time. Calmness is before time. Calmness is a state of mind that you have access to in an instant. Calmness is one thought away from chaos. I would suggest to you that you don't have time ***not*** to be calm, given the type and amount of work you do."

A silence lingers amongst the participants after these words. It is a profound silence that gives people pause for reflective thought. Denise lets the silence carry on until Alma speaks again. "I'm going to have to let these thoughts marinate." Her comment brings laughter from the group, and Denise agrees that marination is a good idea.

"Once you've reflected on this conversation, let me know what conclusion you come to. You know that marinating tenderizes and infuses flavor. I'll be very interested in learning how wisdom infuses your thoughts."

When you consider both these stories about Josh and Alma, what comes to mind that would be helpful for them to know? Do you ever struggle to find more time? To have more calm in your life? Have you noticed that when you relax, time seems to have a way of extending itself?

Calmness is a natural outcome of engaging your True Self. You have probably experienced having more time, and periods of tranquility where your mind is untroubled. Is that not an indication you can have that state of mind more often? Where does that state come from? If you said, "From within myself," then you are right on target, and have uncovered another coordinate on the map of life.

The Profundity of Canadian Bacon

Good fortune came my way, when I was offered the opportunity to talk with a group of teenagers in a drug and alcohol treatment program. Young people in this program were on probation, with the condition that they participate in daylong classes addressing substance abuse and recovery issues. If they were absent, they would be put into a detention facility. Even with this verdict hanging over their heads, youth in some groups did not show up.

This particular group, however, had outstanding attendance. I thought this was quite remarkable, and commented on it. The teenagers seemed surprised by my observation, and rather skeptical. Several spoke up, saying they hadn't regarded their commitment to the program as significant. "We have to turn up or we get thrown into the Detention Center."

"I realize that," I responded. "But I'm told by the counselors that this specific rule doesn't prevent the kids in other groups from being absent. The fact that you all continue to attend indicates you are using your common sense."

As I emphasized my respect for their dedication, they began to look less dubious, and seemed to accept the idea that their attendance was worthy of acknowledgement. Still, my comment was not enough to rouse much interest.

When I went to visit them, it was a late Friday afternoon, very hot, and the air conditioning in the room was not working properly. The kids seemed tired and lethargic, although they were respectful. They tried to respond to my questions about what they had learned of the Three Principles understanding from their counselor, who was trained in the approach. We made some desultory conversation, but weren't really connecting. I was beginning to think of wrapping up our visit and letting them move on to their next class.

Then I mentioned to them that I was from Canada, lived on a small island, and had flown to the city of Vancouver by float plane, prior to flying on the regular airlines to their city. All of a sudden their interest was piqued, and they seemed to wake up. Then, they asked me a very profound question. "What is the difference between Canadian bacon and ham?"

Well, I just about fell off of my chair. I wasn't sure if they were playing with my head and giving me the run around, or if they were genuinely interested. With a quick glance at their faces, I could see their interest was sincere. I answered their question about the difference between Canadian bacon and ham as best as I could. That opened the door to many more questions about what life is like, living on a small island.

They were amazed that we had no stoplights and only a very few streetlights in the village, none in the countryside. They found it even more astonishing that there wasn't a Walmart or McDonald's. I was quizzed about what kind of ice cream we had in Canada, and we exchanged information about our favorite flavors.

A marvelous conversation took place as we were totally engaged in each other; the energy was healthy and high. I learned more about them in that short conversation than I had thought possible. When I suggested it was time for me to leave, they didn't want me to go. They said they didn't often get a chance to express their opinions, except with their Three Principles counselor. They had found our conversation very stimulating and enjoyable. Their comments touched my heart, and I told them the feeling was mutual.

After the session with the youth in the day treatment program, I visited a group of young girls who were in Detention. A couple of the girls were quite engaged as I began to dialogue with them, drawing them out in conversation. But the rest of the group was quiet and shy.

Although my heart was full after my visit with the kids in the other program, I was feeling a bit weary. After chatting for a few minutes, I asked them if I could put my feet up on the hassock in the middle of our circle. They looked at each other in puzzlement, glanced at the officer in attendance, then nodded and said it was okay. I put my feet up and gave a big sigh. The girls also seemed to relax their posture, and we began to converse again, only this time the tone was more comfortable.

They shared several stories about how difficult it was to be in Detention, but voiced approval of the counselor who talked with them about their inner core. They were intrigued by the notion that they still had innate mental health, no matter what they had done. This was a new concept to them, to see themselves as "good" despite the poor behavior that had landed them in this facility. They told me it gave them hope for the future.

Our time together was very nice and I enjoyed our brief visit. As we left the room, the Detention Officer whispered in my ear that she thought it was a wonderful thing I had done, asking the kids if I could put my feet up on their footstool. She said it was a sign of respect for the girls' living quarters, for their home. I hadn't thought of that at the time; it had just been common courtesy to ask their permission. The D.O. said that as soon as I relaxed, she could see the kids loosen up and start to listen and engage more.

It was such a simple courtesy, yet with such profound results. In both groups, soul met soul, without wasting much time. Love moved in, and the door opened to communication and learning; for me, and for the two groups I visited.

Before I met with the young people, I had been training the Facility Officers, department heads, counselors, and other social service providers. We were at the stage in our program where they were beginning to train the kids in Juvenile Detention.

I was very moved by what I observed in the training group. The helpers are so committed to engaging the intrinsic knowledge of the youth in their care. They have moved past working on the kids' behavior, seeing there are no answers there, and instead are drawing out their wisdom. The staff is seeing that as the kids engage their wise, inner core, their behavior starts to change; slowly in some instances, and dramatically in others.

The Officers and counselors are seeing that in some cases, the youngsters are becoming self-accountable. As the youth learn how their thoughts create their experience, and discover they have an inner logic that guides them, they feel so much better that their behavior naturally improves. They are getting a sense of who they really are, on the inside. Soon, they are released, and carry on with their life "in the free." The behavior modification has taken place naturally, from the inside–out.

As the Officers and other staff get in touch with their own wisdom, they are naturally softening their approach to the young people. The negative attention that was prompted by the adolescents' poor behavior is being replaced by positive attention, with respect for the human spirit. Discipline, restraints, and time-outs are starting to diminish.

The kids are so hungry for healthy attention—for approval for what they've done right, rather than disapproval for what they've done wrong. The Three Principles approach offers them this approval, without any conditions. For the kids to see they are still whole and well inside, despite whatever they've done, is an enormous relief for them. It's a new paradigm in the field of Juvenile Justice.

There are "strength-based" programs currently being used in the social service field, seeking to enhance those who are experiencing low self-worth. Qualities such as self-esteem, confidence and drive are thought to be achieved by "doing" something.

An example of this would be doing a role play in front of others, where, to build confidence, the youngster is required to list all her good qualities. The child may experience insecurity, finding it difficult to think of what good qualities she has. Many feel they don't have any, else why are they in Detention? Innocently, the assignment may be adding to the child's insecurity, rather than building confidence.

Granted, the task might prove helpful in some cases; but because the premise is based on outside achievements to build self-worth, it doesn't last unless it is continually fed by more "strength based" activities.

The uniqueness of engaging innate resources, which are ever present and can be called on to help and guide, is a very new concept, both to the staff and to the adolescents. A young man in Detention said to me, "You know, Ms. Elsie, that stuff you told us about innate health doesn't work."

"Why is that?"

"Because I got angry this morning and ended up in 'time out!'" he said indignantly. "So that stuff doesn't work. I still got angry."

"Let's see if I've got this right. You got angry this morning, right?"

"Yeah."

"Have you not had moments of calm?"

"Yeah, I was calm for about five minutes, then I got angry, so—"

I quickly intervened, "Did you hear what you just said? That you were calm for five minutes?"

"So what? I still got angry."

"Stick with me here. Don't you see that the fact that you were calm for five minutes is an indication of your mental health?"

"Yeah, but—"

"No 'yeah but's' about it! Focus on the fact that you were calm for five minutes. That is significant."

"I don't know about that."

"Just consider it—Ahhh, not another word! Just be grateful for the five minutes of calm. If you focus on the calm, you will extend the calm; if you focus on the anger, you will extend the anger. It's your choice. Both feelings are coming from inside you. What would you rather have, calm or anger?"

Tentatively, the young man said, "Calm."

"Well done. You go for it."

That these young people have something good inside of them, no matter what they have done, is heard with skepticism at first; then with "wishful thinking," hoping that it could be true. Finally, it is heard with astonishment, as a psychological and spiritual fact they are beginning to experience.

When the notion of innate mental health was first introduced to the Detention staff, they considered the idea possible, but perhaps not applicable in every case. What the staff is noticing is that innate health is more probable than not. That is a wonderful place to be; being open to possibility opens the door to actualization.

The changes in the training group and the kids are remarkable to see. Having the opportunity to work with the kids myself brought the power of the Principles to life for me in a way I had not experienced before. It's where the rubber meets the road, where the kids serving their time have a second chance at life—a chance not to revisit Detention, time and time again, looking for attention in all the wrong places, but to see the possibilities in their future.

I met several young people who are in the halfway house, part of Juvenile Probation, who have discovered their artistic talents as painters. Their artwork was featured in a special silent auction, sponsored by some in the business community. When I arrived at this event with a colleague who had invited me to attend, I asked her who the young artists were. She smiled enigmatically, and said, "You'll know when you see them."

I wandered around on my own, admiring the various paintings, and then noticed several young boys grouped together. I went over and asked if they were the artists. Shyly, they nodded their heads. They offered to show me their work, and off we went. Their talent amazed me, and as they explained their work to me, what they were expressing, I was moved to tears. I had to contain myself so as not to embarrass the boys. They were so humble about their work, and couldn't believe that I was so impressed.

A silence fell on the audience as the bidding began for one piece, the showcase of the event. The artist was a young girl from the halfway house. Bidding was fast and furious, and the painting sold for a very healthy amount. The funds went to the art program, providing more materials, canvases, and instruction.

The young girl was in tears as she was brought to the front of the room in acknowledgment of her talent. She wept as she dedicated her painting to her father, who was in the audience, and also in tears. She mentioned her Dad was in ill health, and how grateful she was for his love, support, and understanding while she was serving her time in Juvenile Probation. I don't think there was a dry eye left in the crowd by the time she finished.

Two pieces of art spoke to me, painted by two of the budding artists who had shown me around the event. I offered a bid, and in the excitement, I upped my bid again. I left the gathering, not knowing what the outcome would be. To my absolute delight, I found out the next morning that I had won both paintings. I have them in my office, and will never forget that special evening, seeing the world open up for all these young people. Yes, they were in Detention, but free in their spirits; discovering their artistic talent, and the inner resources they hadn't known they had.

Several of the young people we worked with told us that if they'd had the Three Principles training in school, they might not have found themselves in "Juvy." They questioned why this understanding wasn't being made more available. Some of the youngsters commented that if being sentenced to Detention meant finding out about their inner wisdom, then it was worth it. Hopefully, in the future, it won't take being detained by Juvenile Justice in order for young people to find a better way to live a mentally healthy, productive life.

The lesson that has stayed with me after my time with the staff and youth is that it's not important what you say. Truly, what is most important is the ***feeling*** behind the words. In every case—with the teenagers in the day treatment program, the girls in Detention, the young man struggling with the concept of innate health, the staff of Juvenile Probation—what captures and keeps their attention is the feeling of love, respect, and understanding. The conversation may be about Canadian bacon, artwork, whatever comes to mind in the moment. What lingers and stands the test of time is the feeling, the spiritual essence behind life, and the Universal connection of one soul to another.

Prime the Pump

When I was a child, growing up on a farm in the Canadian prairie province of Saskatchewan, we had a very modest life. There was no electricity, no indoor plumbing, and no running water. We piped our drinking water from a well, sunk deep into the ground. In our kitchen, over a wash basin, we had a small manual pump that you had to "prime", meaning we had to pour water in the top of the pump, and work the handle rapidly, in order for the water from the well to make its appearance.

The water in the well was our lifeline. Without it, we would have had a very difficult time, not only supplying ourselves with water, but of course, the livestock, and in the summer, our vegetable garden, the orchard and whatever else depended on water.

Water was scarce in the summer; often we would run out and have to haul it in barrels, from a small town fifteen miles away. As children, even at a very young age, we recognized how precious water was and never wasted it. My siblings and I would use the same bath water to bathe before we went to town on a Saturday afternoon. Going to town on Saturday was our occasional entertainment, much enjoyed by the whole family.

None of us felt hard done by, because we didn't know any other life. I loved growing up on the farm. It gave me a deep and abiding appreciation for the simple things in life; for nature, for peace and quiet, for the tranquility of being on my own. Growing up close to nature gave me a sense of innate wisdom, although I certainly didn't realize it at the time. Many years later, I understood the deep feelings of contentment I experienced when I wandered freely through the fields and meadows, noticing with a child's wonder the new crocuses springing from the ground in the springtime. I understood, upon reflection, that feelings such as these are a result of connecting to our True Self, our spiritual being.

Did I know how to nurture those deeper feelings? No, I did not. Did I realize how precious those feelings are? Did I understand the practical value of peace of mind, of contentment? No, I have to be honest; I didn't have a clue. The deep feelings came and went. Like most of us, I had times of peace and of happiness, and times of turmoil. I had no inkling how to sustain and live in mental well-being.

Not until I was introduced to the understanding of how we create our experience in life, via the Three Principles of Mind, Consciousness, and Thought, did I have some concept of the power, of the incredible resources we have within us. Did I experience those inner resources? Yes. Did I know how to harness them, how to use them in my everyday life? No.

To bring you back to the point of the story, I had another opportunity recently to learn how important it is to nurture our inner resources, to "prime the pump" of our mental wellness. The analogy that comes to mind is this: Imagine our inner resources as a well, sunk deep into our psyche. We have the ability; indeed, it is our God-given right, to draw freely upon these innate resources.

We also have the responsibility to take care of our inner well, to cherish it, to replenish it, to give our inner well time to fill again with wisdom. I'm not suggesting that the inner well is finite. Far from it. I am saying that our human ability to utilize the inner wisdom is finite. Wisdom is infinite.

Therefore, it seems to me that we need to stop now and then and take care of ourselves. In other words, stop and smell the roses. Is this a cliché? Yes, it is. At the same time, it is a sagacious statement. Do we listen to ourselves when our wisdom is saying, "take a break"? Perhaps we do. If you do, more power to you. If you don't, perhaps this chapter will evoke a response that tells you it is time for you to "prime the pump" of your inner assets.

Too often, we overwork our human capacity to the point where we become inattentive to our core resources. As a child, when it was time to haul water from town in order to replenish our supply, I remember skimming the bottom of the well where little but silt remained, clouding the water. In like manner, when we are dredging the last of our human resources, we are clouding our ability to listen to our wisdom, to think clearly and creatively.

What a blessing when Divine intelligence won't leave us alone! When wisdom keeps sending us signals, telling us it is time to "prime the pump." What a blessing when we finally listen! Time to live, time to just BE. It's unnecessary to "do" anything to refresh your spirit. It happens by simply taking the time to once again realize there is more to life than the physical dimension; more to life than dedication to accomplishing tasks.

I will share with you a point when it became necessary to prime my own pump. I thought I should ***do*** something. I felt like I needed time, lots of time to ***do*** things. I had a list, all kinds of plans. I'd plant flowers and paint the house; I'd pay more attention to my husband, to my kids, to my grandchild. I became exhausted thinking of all I had to do…

Finally, as I slowed down, it became quite clear to me that all I wanted was to BE. Whatever came out of BEING would be absolutely right and appropriate, and that would replenish my spirit.

I did go for long walks with my husband, something we hadn't done for a while. I had forgotten how precious that time was, not saying much, simply enjoying the companionship with each other, renewing our love and commitment to one another.

We walked through the forest along a trail skirting the ocean. Enjoying the sun dancing on the sea, it seemed as if the surface of the water was effervescent, sparkling bubbles, and pure energy being expressed.

We walked across a meadow and at the edge of the field were wild blackberry bushes. The taste of them was like nectar, filled with sweetness that burst with flavor upon the tongue. The beauty of this moment was beyond words. It was pure, simple delight with nature, and with life.

How easy it is to replenish the human spirit. All that is required is a moment in time, to once again acknowledge that we humans are more than the physical form. To accept that there is a partnership between form and the Formless. And with the partnership comes responsibility. It is a great responsibility, but essentially a simple one.

Basically put—the responsibility is to take care of oneself. To care for oneself is caring for Self, which is the spiritual essence of life. We are the benefactors and recipients. As we care for Self, we care for others. The quality of care ripples throughout the world. How, then, can we not take time to "prime the pump"?

Is Happiness Overrated?

Occasionally, I've heard people voice the expression, "Happiness is overrated."Their tone and manner in conveying this sentiment appear dismissive, yet touched by longing; the longing perhaps not admitted, or even recognized, should it be pointed out to them. The deeper connotation of happiness seems to be misunderstood. Happiness often seems to be conditional.

"I will be happy if my child does well in her Masters Math class."

"I will be happy if my spouse pays more attention to me."

"I will be happy if I get that promotion at work."

"I would be happy if I had more time."

"I would be happy if I had more money."

When I first heard the comment about happiness being overrated, it brought back memories of how I used to view happiness. In the past, my happiness definitely was dependent on outer circumstances. After all, it seemed clear to me that if things went my way in life, I would be happy...

When the statement about happiness being overrated was mentioned during a class I was conducting, it gave me pause. I considered the question: is happiness overrated?

As I reflected in a timeless moment, it came to me that we all have different definitions for happiness. It would have been presumptuous of me to say categorically that happiness is not overrated. The best I could do in that moment of clarity was to listen deeply, without judgment, and to be open to dialogue about the observation. This is the conversation that ensued.

"What does happiness mean to you?" I asked Terry, the woman who had made the comment.

"When I hear my friends say they're happy, the comment is always made after something good has happened. We're not all lucky enough to have good things happen all the time. My life is not so good at the moment. My husband has lung cancer and his future is uncertain. My job is on the line because I've taken so much time off work to care for him. Our children live in another state and can't be with me to help. I'm angry and I'm worn out," she declared emphatically. "I don't see much in my life to be happy about."

My heart was deeply touched by her story. All I could do was be still for a few moments as I, and the rest of the class, acknowledged her painful dilemma.

"I don't know what to say to that, Terry. You are the only one who can come to a new understanding of how to be with the circumstances occurring in your life. Certainly, it doesn't appear as if happiness has a place in that situation.

"And yet, I can't help but wonder. Does your anger serve you or your spouse well?"

There was a long pause as Terry deliberated on my question. Almost reluctantly, she conceded that anger did not add any light to her state of mind. "Actually, my husband seems to have come to terms with his illness better than I. He tells me to settle down, that everything will be okay. I think he's saying that to make it easier on me. He's in denial.

"I find myself getting angry with him because I don't think he's taking his disease seriously. He does follow his doctor's advice and treatment plan, but he also trusts his own judgment about including alternative supplements. He seems to have come to a balance between listening to his doctor and listening to his own intuition."

"Your husband sounds like a very wise man. It appears he has found peace despite his ill health."

"As a matter of fact, he has. But he's not the one left with all the caring and worrying to do." Terry looked stricken for a moment and covered her face with her hands. She gave a heart wrenching sob, and then composed herself, "I'm sorry, I didn't mean that," she said in a shaky voice. "But sometimes I feel so lost. On one level I know my anger doesn't help, but I'm not ready to let go of it yet. Does that make any sense?"

I found Terry's honesty and vulnerability remarkable. "It makes perfect sense," I assured her. "It's the personal you struggling with your True Self. Your True Self is always available, offering help and guidance. When the personal self is fraught with worry, it tends to ignore that inner voice."

"You mean that the wiser Self is my innate wisdom coming to the surface?"

"Absolutely; the spiritual You is Divine Mind in action, always ready to be in service, if we allow It to manifest."

Terry's face lit up as if a light bulb had gone on inside her. There was a long, intense moment of understanding. The feeling was palpable. I pointed out to her that her insight was a direct result of being connected to her spiritual core, as we all are. Were she not, there was no way she would have been able to see that her wisdom was there for her to rely on.

"Let's have another look at happiness," I suggested. "Tell me what the word means to you."

She thought for a moment, "Contentment, peace, pleasure, joy, glee, exhilaration." In a split second, Terry's features once again showed anguish. "But I feel none of those things!" she cried, getting wrought up again.

"Did you feel peaceful for a moment when you had the insight about your wisdom coming to the surface, allowing you to recognize that your anger was not helpful?"

Her face visibly cleared, the shadows lifting, as she was reminded of her flash of clarity moments ago. "As a matter of fact, the insight did give me some solace. I was feeling so frustrated. When you pointed out that my wisdom was still working, despite resentment of my husband's illness, it felt like an enormous release of mental baggage." Terry hesitated, "But the feeling of relief goes away so quickly," she lamented.

"Not to worry. The fact that you experienced the mental respite, even momentarily, is evidence that your innate wisdom is present. That knowledge will help you sustain your peace of mind."

Another voice from the class spoke up. "My name is Emmett. I've been listening with interest as you two conversed. I hope you don't mind if I add my two cents' worth?"

Both Terry and I spoke at once, "Not at all. Please do."

"Terry, your story is so relevant to what I've gone through with my wife, Shauna. She also has cancer, but is in remission now. However, for the last three years, we've had quite a battle; both with the disease and with our understanding of how to still have a life. Despite her remission, the long-term prognosis for Shauna is not positive.

"What we discovered is this: we are more than whatever disease we may have. This understanding did not come easily to us. Shauna is the one who really saw with clarity that she wanted to live with as much equanimity and grace as she could. She came to this understanding naturally. I, like you with your husband, thought she was in denial. But, I came to see that she was choosing the wiser course; living to the fullest for as long as she could. She wasn't letting the disease dictate her life.

"For me, it wasn't until a friend recommended I take the Three Principles course that I began to come to grips with how our thinking affects any situation in a positive or negative way. With Shauna's support and encouragement, I began to see a positive side to the devastation that had visited our lives. I realized that my anger and depression were not helping Shauna or me; that these emotions only made things worse for both of us. Even when I tried to subdue the negative emotions, or to pretend they weren't there, Shauna could feel the distraught energy from me and it affected her. When her mental energy was low, her cancer was worse.

"When I began to understand that my thoughts create my emotions, both positive and negative, I realized I had a choice in which emotions I continued to entertain. I can't tell you how helpful this knowledge was to me. It was a pivotal moment in my life.

"I won't say that I never have any anger or despondency any more. I can tell you that when those feelings come upon me, my new perspective has brought some relief. I don't feel alone. I have an internal support system alerting me to the fact that my feelings come from my thinking.

"Did this knowledge immediately alleviate the anger or depression? No, but it relieved the intensity and length of time I experienced those sensations. And I will say that as time has gone on and my understanding has increased, sometimes my stress slips away without my even noticing. I don't realize the anxiety has gone, until after the fact. I marvel at this!

"For me, realizing that Thought creates experience has dovetailed with Shauna's natural intuition that there is more to life than the physical form; that we are truly spiritual beings. We continue to travel our journey, not knowing the outcome of Shauna's cancer, whether it will return or not. But we've chosen to live life in the moment. In the moment, her cancer is in remission.

"We seldom think about the cancer because we know we are more than the disease, and our life is more than the disease. Mostly, we are comfortable with the unknown, and very, very grateful for whatever time we have. In a way, the cancer has been a gift to us because it has helped us reprioritize our lives and see what is really important. Our relationship is so much deeper, more meaningful, and every moment is precious."

There was a long silence as the group absorbed the depth of Emmett's words. Finally Terry spoke. "I appreciate so much your sharing your experience with me, with all of us,

Emmett. I admit I have a question still lingering in my mind. Is it okay to ask you this?"

"Of course."

"What if the cancer wasn't in remission? What if Shauna goes into Hospice care? That is what I fret about every day, that my husband will get worse."

"I don't know that I can answer that, Terry. We just live our life in the moment the best we can. I know we are stronger, spiritually, mentally and physically, when we live in that manner. We aren't dispersing our energy by worrying and playing the game of 'what if.'"

Emmett paused for a long moment; then looked at Terry with affection. In a gentle, kind voice he said, "I like to think that we would handle whatever comes our way the best we can, and trust that Universal Mind is always available to give us strength and sustenance; just as it is for you and your husband, just as it is for all of us. That's all I can say about it."

Again, time seemed suspended; then Terry went to Emmett and embraced him. "Thank you," she whispered. "Thank you so much."

I don't think there was a dry eye in the room after that. People stood up and went to Terry and Emmett, surrounding them with their love and caring. As I moved toward the group, I heard Terry say, "Well, this doesn't feel quite like the happiness I imagined. It feels more peaceful, richer, a depth of emotion that I've not experienced before. I feel weepy but in a grateful way."

Her gaze met my eyes, "I'm not sure what's happening, but it's much better than the anger I was going through." Our eyes held for a moment in perfect understanding. There were a few shaky chuckles as we broke for lunch.

Fellowship

Snowfall covered our little island in the Pacific Northwest. Salt Spring is considered the banana belt of Canada, having a moderate climate, nurtured with abundant rain. Snow rarely lasts more than a week, so most islanders enjoy the down time, isolated until the snow plows make their rounds on the main roads, sanding and salting to ensure it is safe to drive. Side roads are the last to be done, and occasionally residents are left to make their own way to the main thoroughfare.

Ken and I quite enjoyed the holiday spirit the crisp weather brought to us, going for walks in our neighborhood, admiring the pine and cedar trees, bowed gracefully by the weight of the snow. The air was fresh, invigorating, and redolent with the fragrant aroma of wood burning fireplaces. Our breath came out like puffs of white clouds in the freezing air.

We approached a meadow at the edge of our community, blanketed in white, glistening and sparkling in the sun. The sky overhead was a brilliant blue, not a cloud to be seen. Except for the crunch of our boots through the crust of the snow, there was silence and peace in nature, sounds stilled by the snowfall.

The feeling was magical, enticing us to tramp through the field, treading in the footsteps of people who had gone before. We were grateful for the pathway that had been cleared for us, allowing us to move ahead without too much difficulty, and felt a sense of fellowship, following in others' steps. We managed to walk to a local coffee shop, stamping our feet free of the snow as we entered. Feeling we could indulge after our hike, we each ordered a steaming hot mug of chocolate, topped with whipped cream.

As we warmed our hands, cupping them around the hot beverages, we reminisced about the past year and how fortunate we felt. We had downsized from a large home to a much smaller one, and felt it was the best decision we could have made, freeing us to live a simpler lifestyle. We were beginning a new adventure, our golden years.

We thought about all the people we had met at a recent conference given by Sydney Banks, the theosopher who uncovered the Three Principles. People had come from all over the world, sharing inspiring stories of transformation they had witnessed, both in themselves and in their clients. The multitude and power of these stories gave a feeling of historical significance to the conference.

People were so touched by the message of hope that the Three Principles offer; particularly by the results being achieved in jails, amongst a population many would consider unreachable. The spiritual fact that all humankind is imbued with wisdom, and the ability to make life what you will, no matter the environment, could not be denied.

So many practitioners are doing amazing work in many different fields; medicine, mental health, education, adult and juvenile corrections, substance abuse treatment, the corporate world. All these fields are responding to the same message. We have the power to change, if we choose, from the inside-out.

Shortly after that event, I was invited to be keynote speaker at a Victims' Services conference. I was honored to be asked, and looked forward to meeting new people, discovering new friends.

My topic was, "The Pathway to Innate Mental Health", and the focal point was how to be in service to the client without counselor "burn out." Burn out is an occupational hazard in the victim services field, as it is in many other professions, particularly social services.

My presentation centered on the Three Principles, giving a brief explanation of how we have the power to create our experience of reality. My theme was innate mental health, making the point that we all have the capacity to move beyond any trauma we may have experienced; that we are more than our trauma. I spoke about the protective factor that our innate spiritual resources offer. This protection allows us to work with our clients and to hear their stories, without being devastated by the ordeals they have suffered. Providers refer to such devastation as "vicarious trauma."

Part of my presentation included a short videotape in which prison inmates shared their stories. They spoke passionately of the Three Principles, and the insights they had gained while in jail. They conveyed how these insights had helped them take responsibility for what they had done. They offered that they were able to find solace from anguish and guilt, even behind bars.

Several inmates enthused about the value their Corrections Officers would find, if they too received some training. As I recall, one of them said something like this: "Imagine, if the Corrections Officers found their health, their lives would change. They wouldn't be so stressed out and take their stress home with them to their families. Wouldn't that be cool?" There was a nodding of heads and animated sounds of approval from the other inmates. Clearly, the prisoners were expressing fellowship toward their guards. How unusual and how extraordinary is that?

A married couple on the videotape shared their journey from a troubled relationship to one of contentment and renewed love. The man, a retired attorney, said he had given up after seeking advice from a traditional therapist, and being told it would take fifteen years to resolve their marriage difficulties. The retired attorney adamantly declared, "I don't have fifteen years. I don't want to spend all that time in therapy. I want my marriage to improve now. "

The couple was seriously considering divorce when one of their friends referred them to a counselor trained in the

Three Principles approach. They met with their counselor twice. During that time, magic happened, and the couple found in each other the love that had seemed absent. Their problems appeared to vanish. The woman's voice trembled with emotion as she recounted how she had moved from a state of hopelessness to one of "glee." She said she had never felt glee in her marriage before.

The Victims' Services conference audience was transfixed by the stories recounted on the screen. At the end of my presentation, many people came up to me and mentioned how inspired and touched they were by the video, and by the Three Principles approach. They wanted to hear more. "Is it really possible that we all have innate mental health?"

As the conference continued through the day, I sat in on other sessions, and the term "compassion fatigue" was mentioned several times. Another term for "burnout," I was told.

Service providers sometimes, as a means of psychological protection from their clients' trauma, find they need to mentally distance themselves. When providers take on their clients' psychological burdens, they often end up experiencing compassion fatigue, because they are emotionally overwhelmed. If this occurs, the counselor's compassion may not be available to help soothe the client. Their rapport with that client will suffer. When compassion and rapport are absent, the healing process for the client also suffers. There is no fellowship in that instance.

Traditionally, service providers are taught to acknowledge their client's trauma, and then move on. In many cases, this is more easily said than done. Without knowing that we have a foundation of wellness, constantly residing within us, moving on can be difficult. And if it is difficult for the service provider to move on, how much more difficult is it for the client? What do we have to offer when we, as providers, are experiencing "compassion fatigue"?

Too often, we are told, innocently, to "acknowledge the pain, feel the pain, and then let it go." This theory is outdated and antiquated. It would be like a surgeon performing surgery without anesthesia. That is what surgeons used to do, before the discovery of ether and other anesthetics. Now, it would be considered inhumane to perform surgery without the aid of anesthesia.

Another analogy: it would be like getting stuck in the snow with your vehicle, and piling even more snow around the wheels to get free. All that process would accomplish is that your vehicle would be more entrenched.

Because human beings have the power to create feelings, when we bring up painful thoughts, we will feel pain. And often times, we will get stuck in the pain, needlessly, without any traction to get out of the cycle. Understanding how we create our experience gives us knowledge; we gain traction, and can move past trauma.

We comprehend that although trauma does happen, it is the way we view the trauma that will make the difference between being stuck, or being able to move on. We can't change the trauma. We can change how we view it. At that point, it doesn't make sense to bring up the painful thoughts in order to get rid of them. Again, it would be like piling more snow around your tires, trying to get out of the rut.

To bring up hurtful thoughts from what went on before, believing this will relieve the pain, brings to mind something Sydney Banks has said: "Going back into the past is like going back into the shower to dry off."

I echo his statement. Don't pile more snow around your mental wheels.

Understanding will melt the snow and move you forward without stress. Success without stress is our birthright.

I am exceedingly grateful for the pathway that Syd has laid out for us, for the fellowship he has extended to mankind by uncovering the Three Principles. May wisdom guide us in extending our fellowship to others, beginning with those closest to our hearts, and expanding out to unknown neighbors across the globe.

Final Words

I started this book acknowledging Sydney Banks and his gift to the world: the Three Principles. It seems fitting to end it by honoring, as best I can, his legacy.

The miracle that happened to Syd in the mid-seventies has yet to be recognized by the global community. Someday, I know, this will occur. The magnitude and significance of his epiphany will help the world beyond our comprehension at this point in time.

All you have to do, to see the truth of this, is to look at the extraordinary results in the many crime-ridden communities where the Three Principles were introduced. Or you may consider the numerous jails and prisons where miracles took place, thanks to the books and other materials of Sydney Banks, shared in conjunction with Three Principles education.

Catching a glimmer of these Principles has changed the lives of people seeking freedom from addictions, couples seeking help with their marriages; has helped teachers better serve the children in their care, and the list goes on and on. People in every segment of the population have been touched by Syd's uncovering these precious gifts, hidden deep within.

For more than thirty-seven years, Syd was tireless in serving humanity with unfailing dedication, boundless love and infinite hope. He felt that if even one soul was helped, it was worth it. He gave his all; at the end, he even gave his health.

In the last few of years of his life, as his health was failing, I saw Syd become more passionate about preserving the purity and integrity of the Principles. He could see that, innocently, some were moving away from the pathway, guided more by the form than the Formless. He had no time to waste and was adamant about sticking to the Principles. Unquestionably, he knew that was where the power of lasting transformation lay. Time and again, he would say with such earnest, loving direction, "Stick to the Principles. They *lead* you to wisdom."

Syd was one of a kind, a great luminary, who showed us another dimension of life. He has left a legacy of hope for all of us, without thought of personal recognition. His driving force was to serve humanity.

When he passed away on May 25th, 2009, countless people mourned his loss. I, personally, felt that a pure beam of light had gone from the world. Ken expressed it as, "The world has lost a treasure."

Syd was an unsung hero, a modest man, with an extraordinarily generous spirit. In his generosity, he showed us, again and again, that the pathway to finding what we seek—our True Identity—is to look within. It is up to each of us to uncover our own inner wisdom. In such a way will the human spirit be lifted and inspired; in such a way will Sydney Banks' legacy of the Three Principles be honored and fulfilled.

Made in the USA
Lexington, KY
02 December 2011